100

Creativity

Ingredients

Everyone's Playbook to Unlock Creativity

Pearl Zhu

ISBN: 978-1-3655-0468-6 (SC)
ISBN: 978-1-4835-9074-5 (e)

Contents

Introduction

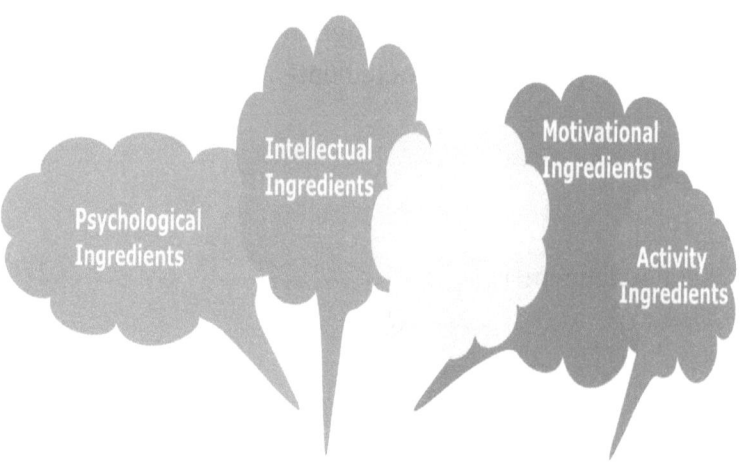

Figure 1 Creativity Ingredients

All humans are born with raw creativity ability. Creativity has many dimensions, with multi-faceted truth and myth, manifold knowledge and multidimensional insight.

Creativity is the ability to create novel value and make a difference; the creative mind is defined as originator mastering "out-of-the-box" thinking to break through conventional wisdom.

Creativity needs a problem to switch on the "light bulb power," and the creative person needs a purpose to fuel positive energy.

Creativity is infused with an inner cohesion and comes from a vision of uniqueness.

Creative person's spirit and soul dance with passion and imagination; creativity needs encouragement as food, and conflict to spark it.

Creativity adds a signature or aesthetic sense that elevates passion to purpose and fancy to enchantment.

Creativity is wings of our mind and tempo of our heartbeat. Creativity is a constructive disruption, not so bad addiction, and a sensational phenomenon.

Creativity habit needs to be cultivated via continuous practices, creativity muscle needs to be strengthened via daily grinding, and creativity excellence can be achieved via persistent pursuit.

Creativity formula has many unique ingredients, read this book **"100 Creativity Ingredients"** to figure out.

In recent years, creativity has become a very highly valued skill, and many think it is the #1 most wanted professional capability in the digital era. We all have unlimited creativity potential and intrinsic ability to think outside of the box, but we need to learn how to unlock it. Creativity is a function of imagination, multidimensional thinking, knowledge, psychology, activities, and motivation. The purpose of **"100 Creativity Ingredients - Everyone's Playbook to Unlock Creativity** "is to classify, scrutinize, articulate, and share insight about one hundred special creativity ingredients, to paint the picture with them, to add colors on them, to embed the music into them, and to make the story via them, in order to unleash our collective creativity potential.

Chapter 1 Intellectual Ingredients: Creativity is the high level of thinking. Thinking is probably one of the most difficult things for human beings, the thinking capability well defines the difference between human and other creatures, and the level of thinking may also well reflect who we are.

Chapter 2 Psychological Ingredients: If you consider being creative as a way of thinking, of imagining, of expression, of perceiving things, of inventing, of inspiring, etc., then it happens every day, multiple times a day. To gifted creatives, being creative is something that they are, whether they're consciously being creative or not. It is the psychological state of the mind depending on what you consider creativity and being creative.

Chapter 3 Knowledge and Capability Ingredients: There is a philosophical connection between knowledge and creativity. Knowledge is path-dependent. This means that to discover an opportunity, you should have previous knowledge in the field to be able to get recognized. Imagination is also needed to be able to apply this previous knowledge to the different context. Nowadays creativity is an important professional capability, and the multitude of professional capabilities can enforce creativity as well.

Chapter 4 Activity Ingredients: While we each have the enormous creative capacity, our willingness to exercise and express it becomes more complicated. Creative people are inspired to think and work nearly every day on creating, not reactively waiting for the "Aha" moment, but proactively stimulating the new energy with the fountain of creativity.

Chapter 5 Motivational Ingredients: Creativity has many forms and manifestations. Take the standpoint that creativity has its starting point within an individual. Creativity can manifest in a collective environment. While the individual contributions provide the 'building block" of creativity, it is the collective consensus on what to do with them that is exciting.

The people who helped to shape our world are some of the broadest and innovative thinkers. Creativity seems to be the free flow of life force energy. It is a wellspring we can learn to tap. Creativity is like a color spectrum. There are commonalities that are relevant to all colors which reflect the spectrum of light. Such metaphor connects the dot back to the nature of creativity. Creativity is innate with many special ingredients; and creativity can be developed if the conditions are right and there is knowledge, love, inspiration, encouragement, and permission. Creativity is a long-term endeavor. Creativity can be abundant.

Chapter 1

Intellectual Ingredients

Creativity is not a "thing," it´s a process that happens as a proactive mental activity to a problem.

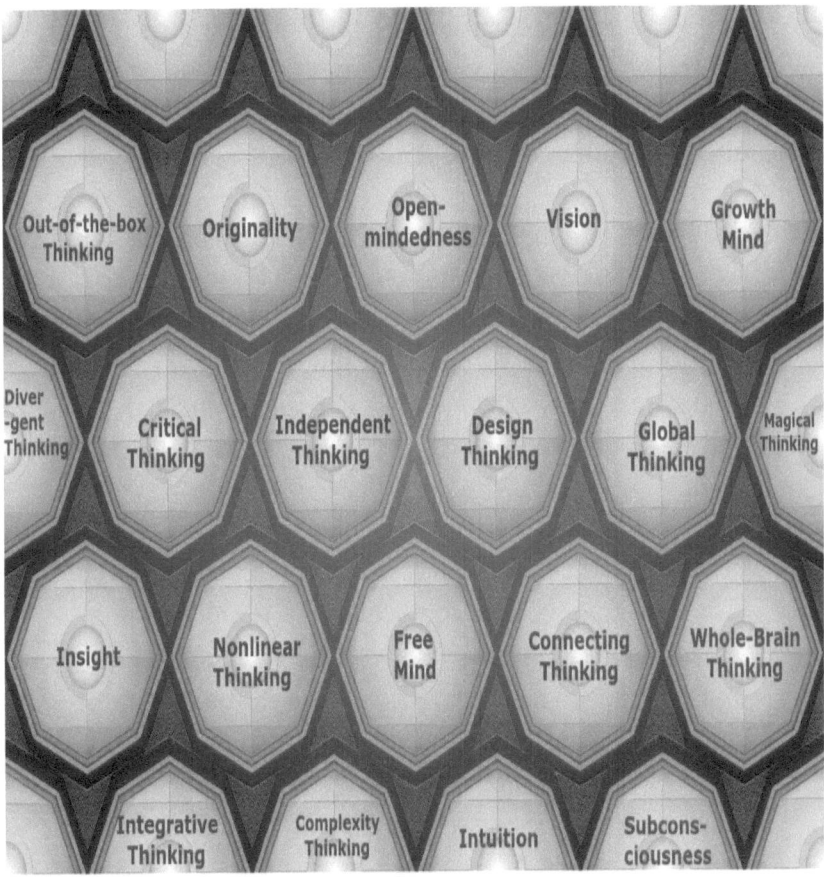

Figure 2 Intellectual Ingredients

Creativity is as much defined by the problem as by the capacity of the individual to connect things to resolve that problem in new and sometimes unexpected ways.

The nature of consciousness is important in creativity. Creativity involves birthing something into existence which was not there before. This involves consciousness of a high order. Creativity is the high level of thinking. Thinking is probably one of the most difficult things for human beings, the thinking capability well defines the difference between human and other creatures, and the level of thinking may also well reflect who we are.

We've been living in the world full of mystery, the things we know, compared to those we don't know, maybe just a tip of the iceberg. The creative people should have a high level of intelligence so that this longing can be converted to thought which has the capacity to explore unusual pathways.

Creativeness also derives from one's ability to let go. Let go of assumptions and stigmas we place on objects, ideas, functions, and has a vision of purpose besides what is already obvious. The willingness to fail and try again in order to one day succeed. The person should have the capacity to enter into moments of reverie during which his/her frustrated thoughts, unanswered problems etc., get reordered, and receive an insight.

The creativity can be sparked in an epiphany or it might be a work in progress. Once we start to formulate an idea, it can lead us to make connections with other experiences we have had in our lives until we finally have an accomplishment we are satisfied with.

1

Out-of-the-box thinking

Thinking out of the box means you are in a continuous learning mode.

Out-of-the-box thinking or thinking outside of the box is the metaphor that means to think unconventionally. When someone asks you to "think outside the box" - they're telling you to throw conventional wisdom and pure linear logic out the window for a while and to let the creative mind run free for a while.

The box is anyone's comfort zone that things are ok and everyone agrees and has the same or similar thoughts. It's a boring tiny space with very little innovative thought contained within the box. In fact, everything in the box is easy to turn stale and stagnant. Great things don't happen inside your comfort zone or in a box; typically, it's associated with convention within context.

"The box" is a mental construct made up of personal (self-imposed) and environmental (culture, parental influence, society) components that one operates within, so thinking outside "the box" means doing something outside of the confines of the construct, in a new and innovative way.

Thinking outside of box means you are in a continuous learning mode. When people leave conventional thoughts and standards to seek additional knowledge and experience, they are stepping outside that box to unfamiliar territory. The resulting ideas wouldn't be completely usable yet - but would serve as a starting point for logic to return to see which ideas could be used. In short terms, this is "brainstorming on steroids."

*The **RULEs** for out-of-the-box thinking*: We all should broaden our points of interest and try new things to extend our thinking box. That leads to a better mutual understanding and more advanced society among all humans.

2

Originality

Original Thinking is unique with an inclination to search excellence.

Originality is the ability to think creatively and independently. Originality is valuable as authenticity. It is not easy to recognize "original thinker," and it becomes more difficult as most of the modern people are too busy to even think and observe. Who are the original thinkers? What might be the traits, dispositions, and motivational orientations that help us to be original in our thinking?

Original Thinkers are those come up with conclusions and solutions for problems with their own unique brain processes. Have the courage to use your own intelligence! It is, therefore, the motto of the enlightenment. Nearly all thoughts come from some sort of internal or external stimulus. Thus, the seeds of original thinking may come from the unoriginal input, but it's a dot-connecting capability to synthesize the unoriginal input into unique output, which makes one an original thinker.

Originality is valuable as authenticity. Be true to one's own personality, spirit, or character. Consider authenticity to be a positive outcome of enlightened and informed motivation rather than a negative outcome of the rejection of the expectations of others.

The **RULEs** _for original thinking_ are: Original thinking is a tough job and recognizes original thinking is equally tough if not less. It is like seeking the treasures. The points like motivation, characteristics, personality, and confidence can be the indicators of original thinking. It can be done if someone remains conscious, alert and has the inclination to search excellence. "Originality is independence, not rebellion; it is sincerity, not antagonism"
- George Henry Lewes

3

Open-mindedness

All snowflakes have different patterns - cool, metaphorically speaking, all snowflakes received are valid and held sacred.

Open-mindedness is about willing to consider different ideas or opinions. It is simply openness to finding connections between experiences, people, things, ideas, etc., and making literally or figuratively something new from those insights.

There is no doubt we live in the digital era with advanced technologies and rapid speed of changes. However, most of the mindsets today which shaped a couple of decades ago in the pre-digital era haven't got updated enough yet. Digital means hyper-connectivity and interdependence; the industrial mindsets favor silos and status quo; digital means flow, the industrial mindset prefers static thinking. The highly creative people are open-minded to always look for the new piece of knowledge or the flash of insight.

The creation bears its own signature of truth which is communicated in time from mind flow. This could be called intuition, but in fact, it is a state of not knowing and open to new adventure. To every question is more than one answer. To every answer is a plausible other question you don't know. You only know what you already know, but the next moment is open to all answers and questions you do not know yet. That means, with an open mind, the creation can enter consciousness.

Narrow or closed-mindedness blocks creativity, as to be creative, one's mind needs to be open to new concepts. A strong blockade to open-mindedness is rigid thinking, relying only on how things were done before. If one only looks at a problem or situation based on some parallel or formula of the past, the "options" for self-expression are limited. If the situation requires a new formula or option, rigid thought prevents the ability to create a new expression from manifesting in that moment.

<u>The **RULEs** for open-mindedness</u>. Start with a completely open and untainted mind. Think differently via the nonlinear lens or different angles. Creative people see the old problems from every direction and find different solutions to exceed expectations.

4

Vision

Vision is not fiction; fiction could be a pure imagination; vision is to zoom into the future as if it were closer.

Vision is something you see in your mind. Envisioning is the imagination's inner screen lighting up in the context of where the vision grows. To envision is the focus coming in contact with the natural deployment, grown from the whole envisioning atmosphere you soak in daily life.

 Innovation comes with a foresight to envision a need that others overlook or ignore and a willingness to forge ahead to satisfy visions, in spite of a risk of failure. Vision grows for those who learn to see and enter into the experience of simple perceptual connection with the wide open personal completion into the moment's happening. As one develops full participation at the moment, so does the perceptual envisioning dexterity, expanding reception and reach.

An innovator is often a visionary and a pathfinder. To the innovator, failure is just another opportunity for success. Innovators are at their very heart visionaries who also have the determination, dedication, motivation, and passion. The world needs more of visionaries who can handle the ever increasing complexities and discover the new path for leading digital transformation.

The RULEs of being a visionary: Vision is something you see, others don't, and a visionary mind is able to and not afraid to leverage contrarian views to shape a holistic picture. The most important thing is that you believe in your vision and many follow your vision. A vision re-conceptualizes the future, connects the previously unconnected dream. It fires the imagination and opens the mind to new concepts and ideas. Hence, vision and creativity are often used interchangeably.

5

Growth Mind

Creativity requires openness and growth mind to new experiences and explore new possibilities.

Growth mind is the progress thinking for making continuous improvement. To be innovative requires a growth mindset. A willingness to "not know" and be able to source possibilities in the emergence space, to be curious and receptive to improvisation and experimentation (and failing), from letting go of the current reality to allowing an unknown future state to emerge.

Cultivating growth mindsets is about how to maximize diversity, to be collaborative, and to intentionally disruptive, create the empty space to generate ideation, new ideas, and solutions that we can be provocative, passionate, intrinsically motivated about and courageous enough to implement or execute in new and unexpected ways. Lack of humility, which is a form of rigidity and being closed to new ideas, is indeed an impediment to creativity.

Creativity requires openness to new experiences or opening your eyes to see old things in a new and different way, with the growth mind to explore new possibilities. Creativity starts with a knowledge base, and then openness to new experience or detecting things you didn't know or applying knowledge from other domains to a new one; it results in creativity in the new domain, sometimes in contexts like that you end up being creative by accident. But nothing is an accident really; it comes from a growth mindset.

The RULEs for cultivating growth minds:

Keeping a growth mind and learning from every experience allows you to be cognizant what is creative for you. But, learn to unlearn your experiences, and make learning a lifetime journey to boost creativity.

6

Divergent Thinking

Divergent thinking is that one starts thinking from one point and expands from there to generate more ideas.

Divergent Thinking is a thought process to generate creative ideas by exploring many possibilities and alternative solutions. In contrast to convergent thinking which aims at setting standards and solving a specific problem. Divergent Thinking is creative, multidimensional, and open-ended thinking aimed at generating fresh views, new insight, and novel solutions.

Divergent thinking is that one starts thinking from one point and expands from there to generate more ideas. Creativity depends upon the ability to think across different fields. When the brain can seek out solutions outside of the domain knowledge and make interdisciplinary connections, there will be a greater probability of success in creativity. These are activities that increase activity between brain hemispheres. Creativity sometimes leads to tangible products which reflect the personality of the individual in their response to the problem stimulus and the means for its expression.

Creativity combines effective and cognitive factors where cognition serves effect. Innovative thinking does not happen in response to knowledge. Innovators usually leverage divergent thinking and hunt for transdisciplinary knowledge based on what they need to validate the innovative idea that they have, rather than develop an innovative idea based on the knowledge they acquire in the present.

It is felt that creative cognition is a self-rewarding process where divergent thinking would promote connectivity through the development of new synapses. "The creative brain--revisiting concepts." --Chakravarty A. Med Hypotheses.

The RULEs for practicing Divergent Thinking: The goal for divergent thinking is to create many ideas about the topic. An essential aspect of creativity (individual or group) is the ability to challenge assumptions, conclusions, and beliefs, and to be able to contemplate multiple, even conflicting views of a situation.

7

Critical Thinking

Critical thinking as a thinking capability is a balanced mix of genetics and learning.

Critical Thinking is the objective analysis, reasoning, and evaluation of an issue to form a judgment or decide. Critical thinking requires an ability to be able to not only ask the right questions but rather absorb information forecast potentials; risks/benefits; mitigation and compare and contrast options, facts, the idea of logic and creativity.

Critical thinking can have the potential to be a deeply creative process as well. Get input from people with a broad range of personalities and cognitive difference on the particular matter. Start thinking both in macro and micro way, and try to tie inter-dependencies into the mix and belief, to your core, you still miss "something." It's then that critical thinking will be able to help drive improvement, extend to creative thinking, create new ideas or solutions and make them stick successfully.

Critical thinking is essential for making decisions based on the careful and comprehensive analysis while creative thinking "creates" possibilities. In other words, critical narrows and creative expands. Engaging and believing, is the door to critical thinking. Creative thinking and critical thinking often work in tandem for problem-solving.

The RULES for Critical Thinking: Critical

thinking cannot be defined as genetically inherited only or, can absolutely be taught. It's a thought process similar to the perceptions, all from the human brain. Critical Thinking is situation based and individual driven. Every individual has an individual approach to a situation where the individual may either choose to apply critical thinking or strategic thinking or ignore. In terms of the professional situation too, the scenario applies.

8

Independent Thinking

Lack of independent thinking is lacking in confidence.

Independent Thinking is about making your own mind, not depending on the authority of others for forming an opinion. An independent thinker with high intelligence can observe completely and think profoundly.

In more detail, knowledge accumulation can add quantified and qualified ingredients into one's thought process. However, it won't transcend into a great idea or fair judgment automatically. "Thinking hard, thinking smart, thinking different" takes a good habit and diligent work, in order to challenge conventional thinking and spark creative ideas.

Independent Thinking can transform knowledge into wisdom. We should not react till we have observed completely. The biggest impediment to creativity is not realizing the glorious capacity one has been given to think, to question, to create, and to explore. Exchange of ideas is ideally based on 'thoughtful candor' that leads to mutual learning and better understanding in which all parties benefit.

<u>The **RULEs** for Independent Thinking</u>: Lack of independent thinking is lacking in confidence, intelligence, insight and personal beliefs about one's creativity. Lack of independent thinking, or being easily led, can impede creativity as well. Also, having too much focus on the external environment impedes creativity, as creative ideas arise from deep thought (internal), among other things.

9

Design Thinking

One of the great advantages of design thinking is to have an outside-in view.

At its core, Design Thinking is NOT linear; it is NOT the kind of thinking that got you into whatever mess you're in the first place, it is NOT dedicated to perpetuating the status quo, it is NOT predicated on following a method. There are different tools and ways which you may or may not use to bang away at the issues, but as soon as you start assigning rules and processes, you are back to linear thinking -- but with frills.

One of the great advantages of design thinking is to have an outside-in view, in most situations where the process isn't producing solutions. Design thinking as a methodology intends to loosen up the business planning process and legitimize less regimented tactics, open to a multitude of inputs and influences.

The "methodologies" being put into the design thinking bucket are somewhat unique and previously outside of the business norm, but have the potential to reframe the problem which in itself is a huge contribution. You don't do certain things in a certain order; you just look at things from a non-business-standard point of view until the form emerges.

The **RULEs** for Design Thinking: Design

thinkers aren't afraid to turn things inside out, look at them from underneath, break them down into bits and pieces, paint them purple and orange, shove bit A into bit B, all with no particular expectation that anything defined will happen, but it might be something else and that may push you in a useful direction.

10

Global Thinking

Innovators with global thinking find more viewing spots than the rest, and therefore, they can solve problems in unconventional ways.

Global mindset is a worldview that looks at problems or issues in such a way that a solution emerges through a collaborative multicultural approach involving global psychological capital, intellectual capital, and global social capital. Being "Global" involves a personal intention to focus on global thinking with intellectual curiosity.

Having a global view (both synthetic and analytic view) is most important for it brings the ability to extract only the best and combined things. Able to listen and understand, and to depict whether and how innovation can be favored in a specific environment via empathy and global thinking.

Innovators with global thinking find more viewing spots than the rest, and therefore, they can solve problems in unconventional ways. They find angles to wiggle through where most are unable to even envision a place where there is an angle. In short, innovators obviously think differently-problem-solving is part of their DNA whether it is in the invention, marketing, repurposing something already being there. Look at Super Glue or Sticky Notes, a prime example of a repurposed discovery.

The **RULEs** to practice global thinking: Be both the world changing dreamer with a critical mind, and be a creative "beyond the border" thinker, but be aware that micro-changes can also power big innovations. Be somewhere in the midst of borderless creativity and a revisited de/re-composition of existing ideas.

11

Magical Thinking

Often imagination and knowledge need to go hand-in-hand.

Imagination is the seed to grow innovation. An open mind leads to imagination, and imagination leads to discovery. Discovery is both an event and a process. Imagination blooms at the beginner's mind; they enjoy experimenting and discovering; there's no rule to limit their imagination.

Imagination is the "magic" force to push up and boost creativity. To put the other way, innovation starts with an idea. Imagination can be seen as helping one expand the initial idea and build a set of hypotheses about how the product of the idea will look like, and how the customers will react to it. Sometimes it is not possible to "see" the facts because they exist in different planes. And until you deal with facts from different sources that relate essentially to the same matter, the patterns are not apparent.

Often imagination and knowledge need to go hand-in-hand. A great wealth of knowledge fuels imaginations. This, in turn, becomes things which can be useful. Knowledge is fundamental for making imagination to reality. But without the magical thinking to "believe in the possible," innovation may not happen.

As Einstein creatively put: "Knowledge is limited. Imagination encircles the world." Modern talent wants to beat Einstein's intelligence, understand more about galaxy or universe, and imagination is the only path.

The **RULEs** to fuel imagination: Imagination can shape the vision; such "vision thing" helps one to see the future as if it were closer. Imagination inspires learning attitude. The higher the level at which we are engaged and stimulated to imagine, the more likely we are to take action. Our imagination allows us dream of where we could go, knowledge helps us to understand how and what forces we are dealing with in our journey.

12

Insight

Insight is the deep intuitive understanding of things, and it often breaks through the conventional wisdom.

An insight is the perception of inner nature of things. Insight is the deep intuitive understanding of things, and it often breaks through the conventional wisdom. Insight is the vision through the 'mind's eyes,' the act or result of understanding the inner nature of things or of seeing intuitively in Greek called noesis.

When you learn to create inner space of clarity, calmness in the storming mind of thoughts emotions, sensations, dreams and imagination, insights can be perceived. Too often people may take the easy path, think and work at a superficial level rather than spend the time to understand what is going on underneath. Insight is about penetrating and often sudden understanding, as of a complex situation or problem. An insightful mind has the strength and the willpower to follow the courageous heart, and thus, has the better chance to be creative.

Creativity is a type of "out-of-the-box" thinking, and insight is thinking into the box after thinking out of the box.

Thus, insight takes creativity and reasoning, intuition and logic, the power of acute observation and deduction, questioning, connection, penetration, discernment, perception called intellection or noesis.

The **RULEs** to build insight. The insight of situation requires in-depth understanding. Insight is an understanding of cause and effect based on the identification of relationships and behaviors within a model, context, or scenario. So, insight does not just fuel creativity, it also makes creativity more tangible and embeds creativity with other thought processes to create value and produce the new knowledge.

13

Nonlinear Thinking

Nonlinear Thinking is an out-of-the-box thinking process for solving problems in a creative way.

Generally speaking, linear thinking is a type of logical thinking and nonlinear thinking is an out-of-the-box thinking. From linear to nonlinear thinking could be evolutionary. In the real, physical world, most relationships are nonlinear. As an object grows in one dimension, its surface area grows as the square and its mass by the cube. Most things have limits to their scale; network connections grow non-linearly with nodes etc. Nature is nonlinear; hence, Nonlinear Thinking is an out-of-the-box thinking process for solving problems in a creative way.

The reason linear thinking is in many cases, not so effective for solving the complex problem because there is always a temptation to use simple linear models to understand highly complex, nonlinear scenarios. People vastly underestimate the complexity and non-linearity of the human cognition processes they rely on all business systems. At the beginning, you often make a one-dimensional, linear, list of things to do. At the end when you have gone through the multi-dimensional analysis or process, when everything else is in place you again have a list of what you need to do for problem-solving.

One characteristic of nonlinear systems is that small changes can have large impacts. A small error, inconsistency or change in a system specification can totally ruin its performance. Similarly, achieving the desired impact can sometimes be as the result of a very small initiative or decision. This is the magic of nonlinear systems thinking. If you pick the right thing to alter, you can sometimes achieve enormous outcomes at little or no expenditure of effort on your part. This approach requires great insights and knowledge.

The **RULEs** for nonlinear thinking: Nonlinear thinkers think outside the lines and often use unorthodox methods to solve complex problems. It is a practical thought process to deal with the ever-changing digital dynamic. "Self-direct" learning is the ability to keep building the new and nonlinear skills and shaping multi-layer, recombinant capabilities for problem-solving and innovation.

14

Free Mind

A free mind can make free choices.

If you empty your desire to accept something, your mind will be free. The "desire" is defined as a strong inner urge or an intense feeling of attraction to something. That could be constructive or destructive, not because of the feeling itself, but based on what that attraction or urge is towards.

A free mind can make a free choice. A free mind is proactive and flow; your mind has a freedom to think everything even though someone tries to make you have no thought or impose their thought on yours; and if there's peace in your mind, you know you may make the nature choice through mindful contemplation but free of thought.

A free mind is neither full nor empty; neither over thinking nor mindless; your mind can fly low and high; flow fast and slow; in the shape or shapeless; lightening up or silent down. It can surge above or stay still.

A free mind is like the flowing wave which is open to the new fountain of thought and to absorb the spring of fresh ideas. It can be critical to identify the patterns or strategic to jump into the future; it can touch the ground to permeate into the seashore, or it can splash up to make a momentum.

The **RULEs** for having a free mind: A free mind is an independent mind which can make free choices. If you think just like many others, your mind may not be free; nobody can limit your mind even though someone can limit your body. You can enjoy the freedom of hands even though your feet are in shackles. You can enjoy the freedom of mind even though your body is in the limited space.

15

Connecting Thinking

A connecting mind can spark creativity more effortlessly.

Creativity emerges as one of the most desired qualities for digital professionals, and creativity is all about connecting the dots. Creativity to some extent is the nature of seeing the patterns that already exist, and then being able to predict how they change, and sometimes manipulate them in a direction that fits our needs.

The mind needs to be freed so that it's connected to the rest of the universe and allows ideas to flow through. A connecting mind that is free from the psychological inertia can flow across the boundary for problem-solving. And obviously, a connecting mind is better at dots connection across the geographical or generational boundaries.

On the navigation dimension, a connecting mind has more antennae focused on the trends and what's going on in the world. What'll it impact the next generation? And what group will have more diversity, the cogitative diversity with a different opinion, independent thinking, decentralization, and aggregation?

A connecting mind can spark creativity more effortlessly. Perhaps an essential feature of the creative brain is its degree of both inter-hemispheric and intra-hemispheric connectivity. A connecting mind naturally thinks with the whole brain.

The RULEs for developing a connecting mind.

The connecting mind which can connect dots more freely and seamlessly is most wanted for spurring creativity or thinking holistically. Every problem that we face has a similar or analogous problem in the past, in some other industry or in a leading area. One just needs to find that existing solution and adapt it to the current problems.

16

Whole Brain Thinking

Whole brain thinking is to leverage both parts of the brain to spur creativity and solve problems.

Everyone has the unique thought processes and a set of thinking preferences. That explains why others can think and react so differently to us in the similar circumstance. Even we have the similar brain, indeed, we think so differently. We are what we think, not based on the partial brain, but the whole brain.

We all have the right and left halves of our brain connected by a dense jungle of neurons called corpus callosum that enable the both halves of the brain to talk to each other. The contention that we have a rational left brain and an intuitive, artistic right side is a fable. The human brain function is far too complex to be so simplistic as "half-half," we are designed to be the whole. Humans use both hemispheres of the brain for all cognitive functions.

Psychologists have used the idea of thinking preference to explain distinctions between different personality types. The brain-imaging studies show the brain recruits both left and right sides for both reading and math. Though in reality, there are individual differences in cognitive strengths. Some are more creative; others are more analytical than others.

It is critical to unlocking creativity and unleashing thinking potential via whole brain thinking. Everything is energy and the human condition is the conditional form of our energy signature and it moves from one conditional state to another. The condition of being human is the energy pattern that allows us to take this form and live as humans.

The RULEs for the whole brain thinking:

Creativity is utilizing both sides of the brain simultaneously - creative + activity. The whole-brain thinking is important to build mental agility to thrive in today's digital dynamic. Every state of energy is conditional and must meet certain conditions in order to take that form. The Whole-Brain Thinking can keep energy flow and spark creativity more effortlessly.

17

Integrative Thinking

The integrative thinker develops a stance that embraces, not fears the essential qualities of enigmatic choices.

Integrative Thinking is a thought process to balance the opposing variables. It is a heuristic process, not an algorithm. In short, integrative thinking is the management style we need if we are to solve the enigmatic problems in the new digital millennium.

The integrative thinker develops a stance that embraces, not fears the essential qualities of enigmatic choices. Integrative thinkers practice cognitive learning, and believe ideas can be sorted through based on categorization: "To perceive is to categorize, to conceptualize is to categorize, to learn is to form categories, to make decisions is to categorize." (Jerome Bruner).

Integrative thinking can balance similarities and differences, narrative mode and the paradigmatic mode, sequential, action-oriented, detail-driven thought, paradigmatic thinking, such a mind enjoys creative tensions, transcends particularities to achieve systematic, categorical cognition.

The **RULEs** to practice integrative thinking:

The integrative thinker is a relentless learner who seeks to develop the repertoire of skills that enables him or her to engage the tensions between opposites long enough to transcend duality and seek out novel solutions. Integrative thinkers understand that they are engaged in a creative process that avoids easy path, or formulaic answers.

18

Complexity Thinking

*In business, complexity both drives
innovation and hinders it.*

Businesses are complex, people are complex, and the
digital world we live in is becoming more and more
complex. Complexity thinking means to understand the
intricate and complex nature of the things by not overly
simplifying and look at complexity in different lenses.

There are unneeded complexities and there are needed
complexities. There are at least two ways to look at
complexity: The first is to try to analyze what the impact of
complexity is on a system (process, business, economy);
the second is to look for the impact of removing some of
the complexity by simplification.

In business, complexity both drives innovation and hinders
it. When a business becomes overly complex and people
get frustrated and annoyed by not being able to accomplish
things easily, this drives the search for simpler concepts
and methods, which is the need to take the innovative
initiative. At the same time, however, over-complexity in a
business may be hiding simple and innovative ways to
achieve things because the people involved just don't get

the time to step back from the complexity and hence, they continue to follow the old routine to do the things, lack of the out of the box creativity.

Valuable complexity brings innovation advantage, such as design complexity that competitors cannot imitate easily; or the collaboration complexity that makes people more productive and business agiler to adapt to the changes. Usually, innovation either through need seeker or technology driver is the key factor to weave such complexity in order.

The **RULEs** _for complexity thinking_: Creativity is the complex, multifaceted thought process, and high-level thinking; and the very purpose of creativity is often to simplify complex things and make them more intuitive. Being sophisticated to understand things with profundity, but follow the simplicity principle to inspire creativity.

19

Intuition

Intuition is often conceived as a kind of inner perception, sometimes regarded as lucidity or understanding.

Intuition is often called as "gut feeling," sometimes, not just the emotional side of the mind, or a "fast thinking" scenario, it's an inner calling, you have to have both sense and sensitivity, listen to it, learn how to liberate self and come up with a new approach to the problem.

Intuition is one element for our unconscious process which is created out of our distilled experiences. An intuitive mind has the strength and willpower to follow the courageous heart, and thus, has the better chance to be creative. Intuition is a deeper sense, should be taken as a new insight, a new idea, and a new angle. Then you are courageous enough to follow the gut and curious enough to understand the surroundings.

Many may think intuition is opposite to logic, but more precisely, an intuitive mind is a complementary thinking process to rational thinking. So, intuition is the quality or ability to have such direct perception or quick insight. It's a subconscious mode of evaluation that can help better understanding the so-called "reality," in which we operate, maximize our engagement with the broader and deeper aspects of our mind and our experience.

Intuition is a deeper sense which gets activated only if we are aligned with nature and the present. Some say it helps us to make connections between events to understand a chaotic world, and others suggest it's necessary for us because we must have some immediate perception of events. Intuition is about "gut feeling" and "thinking fast"; and to be creative, you need to be conscious and curious about surroundings. Intuition is thus often conceived as a kind of inner perception, sometimes regarded as lucidity or understanding.

The **RULEs** for Intuitive Thinking: Everything has pros and cons, intuition can help you "think fast," but pay more attention to the unconscious bias. "Thinking fast," and "thinking slow," need to be balanced wisely, in order to leverage intuition for spurring creativity, but avoid pitfalls and blind spots.

20

Subconsciousness

Subconsciousness is quick and efficient and sometimes can spur creativity.

Creativity is a combination of something currently non-existent, thoughts, and acts and with or without constraints. To be creative, you need to be conscious, curious about things that surround you. To be conscious is to be aware and engaged with both the inner world of thought, feeling, choice, and the exterior world of experience and relationship. The interaction between these two parts of our existence is the home of our creativity.

The condition of being human is the state of mind - unconsciousness, subconsciousness, consciousness, or people can elevate themselves to a 'superconscious' state of mind which will be able to think not only of what exists (subconscious), how they exist in this world, being in the world (conscious), but also how could one possibly apply self in this world to change it, willing to act on how you see things as they could be (super conscious). What is one state of mind to one person does not necessarily mean the same thing to another. And that's where the conflict comes in, and further ignites creativity.

According to social constructionism, the mind would more be between people, in their interaction, with both hard reasoning (analytics) and soft touch (emotion) to hopefully spark creativity. It might start getting far easier if we assume the mind as an emergent property is created, millisecond by millisecond, partially by the brain and partially by its environment.

The **RULEs** for understanding subconscious minds.

Our subconscious mind can do "multitasking." It has the thinking capacity to produce the creative ideas for the disparate tasks or even brings those precious "Aha moments." Subconscious thinking is often quick, and efficient. Using that form of thinking, people perform tasks without being aware of what has been done but sometimes can spur creativity.

Chapter 2 Psychological Ingredients

There is an emotion life cycle in creativity and innovation life cycle!

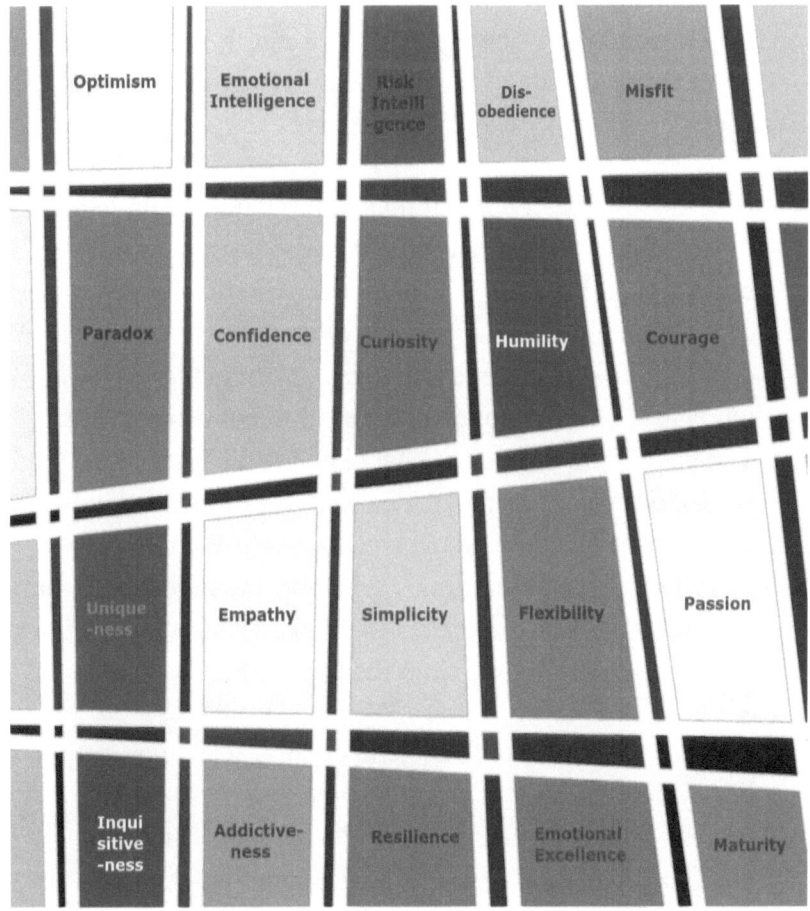

Figure 3 Psychological Ingredients

If you consider being creative as a way of thinking, of imagining, of expression, of perceiving things, of inventing, of inspiring, etc., then it happens every day, multiple times a day. Creativity is innate. If the conditions are right and there is love, inspiration, encouragement and permission, creativity can be abundant. To a gifted creative talent, being creative is something that they are, whether they're consciously being creative or not. It is the psychological state of the mind depending on what you consider creativity and being creative.

Historically, creativity and innovation would seem to have emerged with an instinct for survival, such as inventing basic tools for hunting and gathering. So, there's a connection, with emotional equivalents, for surviving each day. Psychology either encourages or discourages innovation, the ease or difficulties inherent in surviving: Too easy? Too difficult? What elements did past civilizations possess that added to innovation? And how can innovation continue to drive the progress of human race? Greater leaps are found when we move forward from agriculturally based societies to the industrial age, and now slowly, but steadily step into the Digital Era.

There is an emotion life cycle in creativity and innovation life cycle! The kind of emotions within a person that triggers an improvement/innovation process can be numerous and most likely will be a combination of emotions! Certainly, when you think that every rational thought is linked to emotions and creates a feeling. This is an ongoing process just like the feeling to improve and to create.

21

Optimism

Being optimistic is the view looking for the best, coming with "never give up" attitude.

Optimism is the tendency to believe, expect or hope that things will turn out well. It is the right attitude to inspire creativity, explore new adventure and experiment new ways to do things.

Optimism comes from the Latin word Optimus, meaning "best," which describes how an optimistic person is always looking for the best in any situation and expecting good things to happen.

Optimism is an outward view to see the bright side of the things. Being optimistic is the view looking for the best, coming with "never give up" attitude which fuels creativity. Your behavior, the way you showcase your attitude and mood others to put on their thinking cap.

Optimism is looking on the bright side of a situation (external), whereas, being positive is looking on the bright side of all (internal) and reflecting that positivity outwards for others to benefit from and add to.

Optimism shapes a possible mind, a childlike state, anything is possible. By definition an idea is "Possible," that is a step beyond "Plausible," and it does take a mind geared toward innovation to take the concept from plausible to possible.

The **RULEs** for optimism: Optimism is like the gas pedal; passion can give it a push to fuel creativity. Optimism is built on a positive perception or a belief linked to one's expectations some of which may take the time to turn creative thought and ideas into the reality.

22

Emotional Intelligence

Emotional Intelligence is the ability to identify and manage your own emotions and the emotions of others.

It is our creative mind that sets us apart from the animal kingdom and has given us the creativity to improve our lives. Higher Emotional Intelligence helps you have an open mind, minimize biases, be cautiously optimistic, be an effective listener and be more creative.

Emotional Intelligence is the ability to identify and manage your emotions well. It includes emotional awareness - the ability to identify your own emotions; the ability to harness emotions and apply them to tasks like creativity; and the ability to manage emotions effectively. The inhibitor to creativity is overextension and physical/mental fatigue. Emotional problems such as stress and sadness, or vice versa, can impede creativity as well, depending on what emotions inspire the individual, and what emotions don't. If an individual is also plagued by self-doubt, then he or she would be even less likely to assert a creative idea public.

Emotional Intelligence is a tool to live a life with balance. Intuition, idea generation can be in mind which is free of turbulence and has the knack of achieving balance. The minds with high Emotional Quotient (EQ) can take "tough decisions keeping their sensitivity intact." They will focus their strength and excellence in creativity, rather than divert their energy towards negative competition. Such minds are more objective, creative, accountable, empathetic, intellectual and progressive.

The RULEs to nurture a high EQ mind.

Creativity exists in all fields. A high-EQ mind can turn on creativity switch more easily. Now with conscious thinking, tools, and techniques, even emotion can be managed more scientifically. For that, one would have to go deep within. Going deep would touch the metaphysical aspects of a human being.

23

Risk Intelligence

Innovations succeed when failure is seen as a learning step to great success.

Creativity is inherently risky because it is new and different. Anyone or any organization that fervently wants to be creative must be willing to face risks, and overcome the fear associated with such risks.

However, people tend to be "risk averse." Fear of change both personal and in organizations, fear of disruption, the existence of chaos, etc., are the very obstacles to stifle creativity. To be innovative, people need to overcome fear, have the right dose of courage to pursue creativity.

With creativity, "change" is made." With every "change," the risk is involved. The more dramatic and powerful the change is, the greater the risk would be. Finding an alternate route around a road block is a creative act though many people would not recognize it as such.

It's easier to think and act creatively in an environment that encourages risk and nurtures creativity. Innovations fail because folks fear failures. Innovations succeed when failure is seen as a learning step to great success.

The **RULEs** for encouraging risk-taking: You have to remember that innovation can be a breakthrough and notice that it requires a "break." They include being a risk taker, challenging the status quo, being fearless, looking at failure as a learning opportunity, and always looking for a better way.

24

Disobedience

Dissatisfaction with status quo is the psychology behind creative disruptions.

Creative people tend to be non-conformists, or, at least, appear to be. However, that is just the way they think, not really intentional. Creative people judge the world for themselves and they are skeptical of but open with outside opinions.

Creative people define and create their own convention that they live by in comparison to others who just accept or inherit their convention to live by. The problem of creativity is never to get new, innovative thoughts into your mind, but how to get old ones out. To understand why you have to go against the status quo is then going to allow you to know if it is necessary to go on or not search. This intuition is doubled by the courage and "opportunities."

Creative people are impatient with the status quo and believing there is always a better way to do things. The next focus must be ideation which can be implemented and not just great wow ideas which one cannot implement.

The **RULEs** of disobedience in a positive

sense: Dissatisfaction with status quo is the psychology behind creative disruptions. The profile of the creative that is most common and necessary is rare being with an innate curiosity to improve, at the risk of disobedience in a positive sense. It's about the desire to make something better and the willingness to try. **There's no innovation without disobedience (French Proverb).**

25

Misfit

Being "misfit" with advanced thinking and forward-thinking influence is a digital fit.

We have to remember that as each one of us is an individual, each is a misfit in some way or the other. To put another way, shall you fear if you are "too" fit in a stereotype - fear of being a misfit is a closed mind to keep status quo.

So being called misfit is really not alone, and perhaps a compliment, and more possibly, the misfits have more advanced mindsets, creativity potential and forward-thinking influence than the mass, and they are the innovators with the real digital fit.

Pioneers were considered misfits, and where would we be today without that spirit? Misfit has a raw intelligence to think independently, creatively, critically or futuristically. Most creative people are off the beaten track with their ideas and that is what makes them unique and sought after. Entrepreneurs, scientists, artists, musicians, teachers, etc., all can be considered misfits. And more critically, such 'misfit' characteristic decides whether you are an authentic leader or a follower.

Often, it's fear that stops you from being creative; and fear takes many forms, fear of change, fear of the unknown, fear of rejection, and all that you have come to know. Sometimes you may have learned it was unsafe to express yourselves, and you have to relearn that it is safe to do so. But when you always play safe, in afraid of being different, you may tarnish the character or lose the creativity. Either you are a round pit cannot fit into a square hole or a running river cannot keep still, misfit can be a real fit when time flows.

The **RULEs** for "Dare to be a "misfit": The world has too many stereotypes, we need more rebels, generally, not running after a single cause! Rebels without a cause are the need of the day. There is the beautiful gift called life didn't come with any instructions, but we can remember that we are all in this together, all doing the best we can, and that it is ok to celebrate ourselves, express ourselves, forgive ourselves, accept and most importantly to appreciate ourselves, and then we can also cultivate the empathy to appreciate others, understand others and enjoy the nature of diversity and unlock our collective creativity.

26

Paradox

The paradox is a situation, person, or thing that combines contradictory features or qualities.

The paradox is the result of two opposing truths existing side by side, which can be both right. The paradox is like the two sides of the coin, they are not just opposite, but also complementary, to make it a whole. To deal with paradox and cure superficiality, the old cliché comes to mind: two sides to a coin; one complements the other.

Paradoxical intelligence is emergent as a type of critical intelligence to deal with today's VUCA (Velocity, Uncertainty, Complexity, Ambiguity) dynamic. It is the process to define as a statement that seems contradictory, unbelievable, ambiguous, that may be true in fact, and you can think through multi-dimensional angles to gain cognizance.

Innovation has the characteristic of paradox, and often creativity is sparked by conflict. Creative outcomes may come from recombining ideas in different ways to create the fresh ideas or the new ways to solve old problems. Digital now is just like the new window, provides a multidimensional view of hyper-connected nature to see things differently and gain in-depth understanding.

Creativity is a divergent-convergent dot-connecting scenario. Interdisciplinarity and paradox are the rare and precious dots to spark the next level of innovation. From innovation management perspective, the mindset with high paradoxical intelligence is better at balancing between orders (standardization) and chaos (innovation).

The **RULES** _to gain paradoxical wisdom_. All wisdom has some paradoxical theme. The digital professionals with paradoxical intelligence are more inquisitive and innovative. The paradox of innovative leadership is about the balancing of asking and answering, leading at the front and leading from the behind, or simply knowing when it's the time to lead, and when it's time to follow.

27

Confidence

Being confident means you know who you are, your strength and your limitation.

Creativity is often an adventure full of risk, and confidence is the personality trait to unleash your creativity potential. Confidence is often a reflection of your innate mentality. Being positive is within yourself, reflects your personality, thought processes put into action. A positive mental attitude is focused on strength, opportunities, to fuel creativity and inspired actions.

Confident people with positive attitude see the bright side; they have a special mindset that rain or shine, leads them to positive outcomes. It is about being your best, not beating another in a negative way. Confidence is not equal to ego or self-centeredness, or arrogance. Ego is actually another major stumbling block to creative thinking.

Being confident means you know who you are, your limitation and what you don't know, so you communicate in a consistent way. If you feel you always need to be the smartest one in the room, you're missing out.

Innovators and innovative leaders have a ridiculous amount of self-confidence. If you're not sure of yourself, you won't be able to convince others to follow your leadership and vision. They have persisted because they were convinced to be in the right direction. And many times, you also must be willing to fail a lot and be very persistent and thick-skinned to make a successful innovation journey.

The **RULEs** to be confident. Be confident means to be comfortable in your own skin. Be authentic to be true to oneself and to the world at all times; to have the ability to know that nobody is perfect but can live a dream perfectly; to constantly unlearn and fight against conditioning and to respond creatively and uniquely at all times.

28

Curiosity

A curious mind enjoys inquiring,
experimenting and discovering.

Curiosity beat IQ in every chance to create the fresh new idea. The clear manifestation of intellectual curiosity is to ask good questions, the open questions, the profound questions and the thought provoking questions. Though there are no such things as stupid questions, framing the right question can stimulate creativity and it is often the halfway of problem-solving.

People with intellectual curiosity are more like to ask those open questions such as "What if," "Why not." etc. It inspires the fresh thinking about the legacy issues, the new angles to see the unsolved problems, the other dimensions to leverage cause-effect. The science of questioning is about asking the right question at the right time to the right person for the right information. And the art of questioning is to ignite creative thinking and critical thinking and stimulate the creative sides of our brains to find answers.

A curious mind enjoys inquiring, experimenting and discovering; there's no rule to limit their imagination. We all know kids are curious, but when people start to be socialized to fit in the surrounding or enter the work as an adult, they place themselves in a different mindset, they start to fear that their creativity will be seen as disruptive, infantile, they live up or down to other people's expectations, they set limit to fall into conventional wisdom, and they just become lack of the curiosity or lock they own creativity potential.

The RULEs to keep curious and keep asking:

If curiosity is a sort of raw intelligence, it can sprout such creative intelligence to spur innovation. And this raw intelligence can be sharpened via continuous learning. Intellectual curiosity leads people to inquire, learn and dig through the root cause of issues, in order to co-solve the common problems and co-create the better world via creativity.

29

Humility

None of us will ever know enough, and that is why humility is a critical component of innovativeness.

Humility requires great self-awareness and deep listening; makes room for others to discover their own insights; or gives room for their perspectives to emerge to the collective wisdom. There are various definitions of humility, the general one is to take our place and give space to others.

Humility means to be humble; it means you understand your own strengths and limitations and will look to others to help you get to your goal instead of going it alone. If you are humble, you are open to learning both about yourself, your team and new ideas. Truly curious leaders are more interested in what they don't know than just providing answers to show what they do know. Listening to others' input with humility to accept it may be useful to facilitate innovation, deep empathy which, in turn, builds trust and respect.

From innovation management perspective, humility is considered one of the most important traits to develop high mature leadership which embraces inclusiveness and encourages creativity. As for the innovative leaders, the more they learn, the more they appreciate how little they know. They encourage open and constructive communication, which leads to continuous improvement. These leaders are the ones who have the skills to lead people from 'within,' not 'above.' They empower their team members, respect their expertise and appreciate every team member's contribution to innovation for the overall success of the organization.

The **RULEs** to nurture humility: Humility allows one to have a learning attitude, be curious and innovative, understand oneself, understand others, and strike the balance of being confident and being humble, self-worth and the worth of others. In this way, one is able to be assertive and stay the course. Not lose focus and allow emotions to get in the way of teamwork and team innovation, and take the continuous innovation journey.

30

Courage

Be courageous to listen to what you don't want to hear and have the guts to be innovative.

Innovation is about thinking differently, acting differently, delivering differently, and adding value differently from the status quo. Innovators have the tendency to constantly question the status quo. Are innovators more courageous, or does courage refine an innovator?

Innovation requires thinking beyond, as opposed to outside the box, altering or changing the frame of reference to create previously unconsidered solutions. Innovators need to rise above the status quo and take on a new set of activities that have them involved in the strategy development process from the get-go. In addition, there is a direct relationship between competence and courage. Put differently, there may be a willingness to act, but an inability to do so. Innovators also have the interdisciplinary knowledge and multifaceted ability to connect unusual dots. Innovators are courageous. Without courage, there is no innovation or innovators.

The opposite of courage is fear. A culture of fear and mistrust drains energy and thwarts creativity. The feeling of fear is a power unto itself. Fear can paralyze an individual to do nothing or become manipulated by the power of fear. Fear will drive you away from your personal goals, your ambitions, and your creativity. Likewise, fear can paralyze a company to maintaining status quo, refusing to adapt to change. It turns to become such a counterproductive behavior when the contribution of others offers the potential to add so much value.

The **RULEs** to be courageous: To be creative, there is a need to do away with the fear of being different. The fear of being noticed, of being laughed at or rejected prevents many from stepping out, taking new adventures, and exploring a new way to do things. At the business level, building a "fearless" working environment means to inspire openness, innovativeness, and critical thinking, and empower talent to unleash their creativity potentials with less fear.

31

Uniqueness

There are no two snowflakes are the same, we are all unique individuals.

Uniqueness is human being's most valuable asset. The only person you can be is yourself. Accept yourself as you are and let others be who they are. We all want to feel loved and accepted and that is only natural, we all want to belong, and we sometimes seek approval. The reality is that not everyone is going to like us, agree with us or think like us! So it takes the time to learn to feel confident to be different, to be unique, to celebrate and be proud of whom we are.

The next step for discovering professional uniqueness is investigating what's your strength, your passion; defining your task, things you want to do and do better than others. The emphasis is on trying to determine which competencies or capabilities should be used in which combination and with what level of weight for each, for every different situation. Improving one's cognitive ability involves exploring varieties of meanings/thoughts, abandoning old connection, and establishing new relations. In neuronal terms, this involves disabling some of the "wiring" and working on the new ones. All of that requires a deliberate mental effort, connects your dots and discovers where your unique value proposition is, and how to become more creative effortlessly.

The indicators to assess the uniqueness and intrinsic creativity capacity of individuals include: Self-awareness (recognition of one's strength and weaknesses), interdisciplinary skills and knowledge, cognitive ability and style, intellectual engagement, creative problem-solving, personality (openness to experience, tolerance of ambiguity, personal initiatives), tendency to constantly question the status quo, plasticity (fast learning), ability to identify patterns, ability to make unusual connections, capacity to adapt, emotional intelligence (risk taking), willingness to accept feedback, or a tenacity to refuse it, etc.

The RULEs for competing with uniqueness.

Either at individual or business level, being unique is to pursue authenticity and build the unique set of capabilities which will help you unlock creativity and achieve career or business goals.

32

Empathy

Empathy is the ability to understand others from their perspectives.

Empathy is about thinking as if you were in the other party's position. Humans aren't as good as we should be in our capacity to empathize with feelings and thoughts of others. Now the physical barriers such as oceans or mountains cannot stop people from communicating with each other, there are still walls built in people's minds and there are knots tiered in their hearts. Those psychological barriers often caused by lack of empathy, become the very obstacle to amplify creativity effect and scale innovation.

Empathy is an ultimate level of human cognition of being wise-understanding, active listening and balancing between tolerance and respect to achieve that. So, to spark creativity and encourage innovation, the greatest contribution to humanity would be taking the time and the sincere effort to understand the other person. Walk in the shoes of the person you're judging, understand him or her from a different angle - character, strength, creativity, consistency, etc.

Empathy is absolutely one of the most critical Ingredients to develop creativity. It means an open mind to understand how others think and value; it means proactively gaining cognizance of your environment and adapt to it; it means appreciating the diverse thoughts and opinions, converging them to capture the new knowledge and insight, and further stimulating creativity.

*The **RULEs** to cultivate empathy*: Empathy is a very important soft skill that is frequently undervalued. It's not born, but can be nurtured. Everyone has something to offer, and it is up to us to allow an equal giving and taking, to kindle creativity and make innovation pervasive.

33

Simplicity

Progress is in simplification, which often follows complexity.

Creativity is a higher level of communicating or perceiving the beauty and balance of nature creation, or what being called the law and source of the universe. Creativity is associated with aesthetics which allows us to see patterns and complexity at an intuitive level, without having to dissect it, as knowledge exceeding known boundaries takes on an aesthetic quality.

Creative thinking is surely complex, but not necessarily complicated! It is more of thinking complexities to simplify them through intuition. The outline might be simple, but the details are intricate! When pioneering and solving problems, initial solutions are often more complex than required, and then adoption and progress come with simplification. Progress is in simplification, which often follows complexity. Either innovation process or innovation itself should move up the maturity ladder from functioning, firm to delight and agility.

Philosophically, simplicity further implies elegance, intuitiveness, and maturity. If you can't explain it simply, you don't understand it well enough. *"The ability to simplify means to eliminate the unnecessary so that the necessary may speak."* - Hofmann

The **RULEs** to advocate simplicity: Innovation is often to figure out the better way to do things. And simplicity is the ultimate level of sophistication. *"**Any intelligent fool can make things bigger, more complex, and more violent. It takes a touch of genius and a lot of courage to move in the opposite direction.**"* - Albert Einstein

34

Flexibility

Flexibility is a mental process which results in an action that tests a possible solution.

Though the meaning of the word flexibility, in general, more refers to physical movement capable of being bent, without breaking; from psychological perspectives, it is about the ability to adapt to changes, the alternative way to do the things; and the resilience to survive or thrive from the failures.

Flexibility is a mental process which results in an action that tests a possible solution. Things either work or they do not. That action is creativity. Flexibility is an important trait of innovation. It is simply about how flexible people can see what's around easily and effortlessly and discover a better way to do it.

A flexible mind loves choices, enjoys making differences; feels comfortable to be unique and welcomes the diversity of thoughts as a fountain of creativity. A flexible mind is not restricted to rigid processes and challenge conventional way to do things. People with a flexible mind can work as a team more seamlessly, but also professionally. Such a team or working environment encourages collaborative thinking, builds adaptability to create mutual interest communities, to identify common, to inspire creativity, to build flexible processes focusing on outcomes without micromanagement and to create a sense of urgency as well.

The **RULES** to be flexible: It's easy to say you are flexible or playful and have a lot of innovative desire, but within the walls of an organization, the overly hierarchical culture still stifles innovation. Flexibility allows an innovator to bend the rules as long as it is not harmful to the organization. As long as this flexibility is provided with necessary oversight by the management, all elements of risk-taking propensity and also proactive behavior will lead towards innovation.

35

Passion

Creativity is a passion for some who are inquisitive and want to explore new possibilities.

Passion is an emotion, which is something that comes from within. However, it is a result of the belief and conviction which can be fueled from without. Passion enables determination, creativity, strategy, and talent. If you do not have the passion for what you do, determination, creativity, talent, and strategy become hard work which in turn disables determination, etc.

People are passionate about different things. We are all different. Where is your passion flowing toward perhaps makes the best clue for discovering "who you are?" Passion is an emotion, which is something that comes from within, the bottom of your heart, with the strong sense of connection with "self," not only the reasoning of your mind.

Following the passion also requires a good sense of judgment that you are on a right path. Therefore, vision is crucial to sustaining passion. Visionary could mean the ability to think outside the box, to think creatively, to be innovative both inside and outside the certain boundaries. Passion is an inspiration which is often accompanied by vision. Passion can sustain and can be the drive to realize visions.

The RULE to be passionate. A passion with a good positive chain of thoughts followed by positive actions often reaps the benefits of innovation and leapfrogs progress. Passion is the inner energy to unlock creativity and keep the creativity fountain flow.

36

Inquisitiveness

The art of questioning is to ignite innovative thinking.

Be inquisitive means you love to inquire and you are always asking questions. The essential to questioning stimulates the creative sides of our brains in order to find answers. The good question is usually open and thought-provoking. It brings multifaceted perspective. Like a piece of art, the great question is beautiful and insightful, to connect the dots and spark the imagination. The art of questioning is to ignite innovative thinking.

Either the big "WHY" question to diagnose the root cause, or the witty "WHY NOT" question to provoke creativity; either the straight "WHAT" question to stay focus or the logical "HOW" question to reach the detail, a good question is half way of problem-solving, a fine-tuned question stimulates energy, a great question inspires imagination and triggers creativity. And a set of excellent questions themselves is perhaps like a poem, both philosophical and intellectual.

The science of questioning is about asking the right question at the right time with the right person for the right information to solve the right problems. Too often, when asking questions, you tend to assume that the people who are answering actually understand your language. Do not get lost in translation. The science of questioning is about clarity, logic, and innovating.

The RULEs to ask good questions: Digital professionals today must become more inquisitive to ask great questions. More often, to deal with today's ambiguity and complexity, framing a good question is more difficult than answering them technically, and a good question is both art and science. *"The important thing is not to stop questioning."* - Albert Einstein

37

Addictiveness

The restlessness to create is a sign of addiction.

Creativity is addictive because it's a kind of a flow - not the repetitive patterns to do the same old things. It could also be a desperate need or habitual actions to keep doing something new. You create one thing; you are on the lookout for creating another; you do become restless if you are not able to. This restlessness to create is a sign of addiction. Creativity comes from dissatisfaction with the existing scenario and understanding the requirement as well as zeal to create or improve the thing.

Creativity is fresh and new every time. The negative connotation about addiction is when you want to repeat the old pattern and seek comfort. You avoid "new." Because it gives uncertainty and insecurity with new and change. Creativity loves the challenge, with the courage to see the new; creativity is fresh and new every time. It does not fear. It has that emotional or affective strength to trust the process of creativity. Engaging in creativity inevitably creates tension, conflict, and emotionally charged debates and disagreements because we need both control and predictability, creativity and change.

Creativity needs encouragement as the spirit of food, and conflict to spark it. Conflict makes the mind think differently leading to creativity. The combination of good chemical balance is reinforced because it does not go for repeating due to helplessness but due to fun and the joy of life.

The RULEs to be addictive to creativity: If

you have to addictive to something, addict to creativity. Creative people are looking for new challenges relentlessly. They don't create out of boredom. They overcome the boredness, and sometimes creativity is to retune the known things into the new ideas. Creativity is to find better ways to do things. Creativity is the discovery of what has not yet been seen nor manifested. Creativity is not an addiction. It is a beautiful phenomenon.

38

Resilience

Being innovative is a state of mind.

At the age of innovation, failure is seen as a fruit full of experience. Failure is part of innovation; it is very much an intrinsic part of innovating. Therefore, resilience becomes an important quality to encourage creativity. Resilience is a "system" (person, organization, whatever) being able to maintain its recognizable essential characteristics in the face of "disruption," that could look like "bouncing back" or it could look like "growing around" obstacles.

Resilience is a property of an elastic component of a person. This indicates the person can undergo high dynamic stress and yet he/she is able to recover smoothly to his or her original situation without much degradation of him/herself. In short, we call this person a tough person in all predicaments.

There are many causes to fail innovation, and be resilient is the right attitude to fail forward. It's about regaining one's footing which could be bouncing back, forwards or restructuring your life integrating the change in some way that works. Innovation is a journey, people need to pace themselves and recognize that innovation is not an on-off switch. There will be ups and downs along the way and you need the resilience to make the trip to completion.

Failure is inevitable, learn from it. Part of the issue of resiliency is how significant the adverse situation is to the person. A tree is still recognizably a tree even if it's all crooked to get adequate light or soil and we can be recognized as "us" even if we adapt to a difficult situation.

The RULES to be resilient: The person lives in a grounded and centered place, being flexible and adaptable in the midst of adversity, threat, and stress. It's the ability to respond to change, be innovative, to recover quickly from setbacks, as well as the capacity to respond to the unexpected in a way that increases gain or minimizes loss. Of course, it's also about being able to keep focusing, even during stress and disturbances, because innovativeness is a state of mind.

39

Emotional Excellence

Emotional Excellence means to have an ability to respond to emotions, and manage them well.

There is an emotion life cycle in a creativity-innovation process cycle. The kind of emotions within a person that triggers an improvement or innovation process can be numerous and most likely will be a combination of emotions! Certainly when you think that every rational thought is linked to emotions and creates a feeling. This is an ongoing process just like the feeling to improve and to create.

We need conflict to initiate, but after initiation, there should be a debate to create! So, different kind of emotions is involved to truly become innovative. The conflict can come from an internal conflict or a conflict with the outside world. The most difficult part is to transform the conflict from within to a productive life cycle. This is wholeness. If you have a stable internal process and you can even help others, then innovation with the outside world will be the next challenge.

The need to solve a problem might lead to innovation, but a need to innovate isn't completely addressing the problem psychologically. There are more situations related feelings that have an impact on you as a person or on your team. What about trust? Or what about happiness? So your emotional well-being has an impact on innovation, but what is triggering your emotions? What from the outside world has an impact? What about the right innovation climate? Your personal climate, your team climate or your organizational climate?

The constructive emotion sustains creativity as well. The patience relates to tolerance and tolerance gives us the ability to understand other points of view; tenacity could help lead to your vision and keep things on track etc. Stamina might be a physical requirement to maintain this tenacity.

The **RULEs** to achieve Emotional Excellence:

Emotional Excellence means to have an ability to respond to emotions, and manage them well; translate emotion into values-driven goals and purposes, unlock creativity and pursue the better way to do things.

40

Maturity

Maturity refers to having a sound understanding of basics and making a fair judgment.

Mental maturity is nothing to do with physical maturity, it is a thinking ability to spark creativity, enhance understanding, and sharpen multifaceted intelligence.

Creativity demands the possibility of the wrong in order to be exploring in a free and playful way. Creativity suspends or defers judgment. However, it doesn't mean creativity is a lack of the principles or mental maturity, the well-set disciplines can streamline the train of the diversified thoughts and the fountain of creativity, and further enforce mental maturity.

Maturity is simply having the ability to live comfortably with contradictory thoughts, having knowledge of talking to various people in different ways, and expressing things creatively to convey the vision; it's the ability to speak courageously by taking care of the feelings of the other person empathetically; saying your part without hurting the others; communicating, but not winning a small battle of ego. It is the thinking and understanding ability which we gain through learning, reflecting and innovating.

Maturity is the clarity of thoughts along with self-control which helps in choosing the most appropriate reaction to circumstances, or inaction - deciding not to react to any given situation. Maturity is the ability to wait, think, and respond to a situation without responding with a knee-jerk reaction. It's the ability to weigh in the impact of what we are planning to do and who will be impacted because of the intended action. So high mature people can set priorities right and focus on creativity-oriented thinking and activities.

The **RULE** to improve mental maturity: A fruit or vegetable is mature when it is ripe, ready for consumption. When a person knows the rules of life and has trained his or her body to great levels of capability or skill such as creativity or problem-solving, the person becomes fully developed and thus has achieved maturity in the role.

Chapter 3 Knowledge and Capability Ingredients

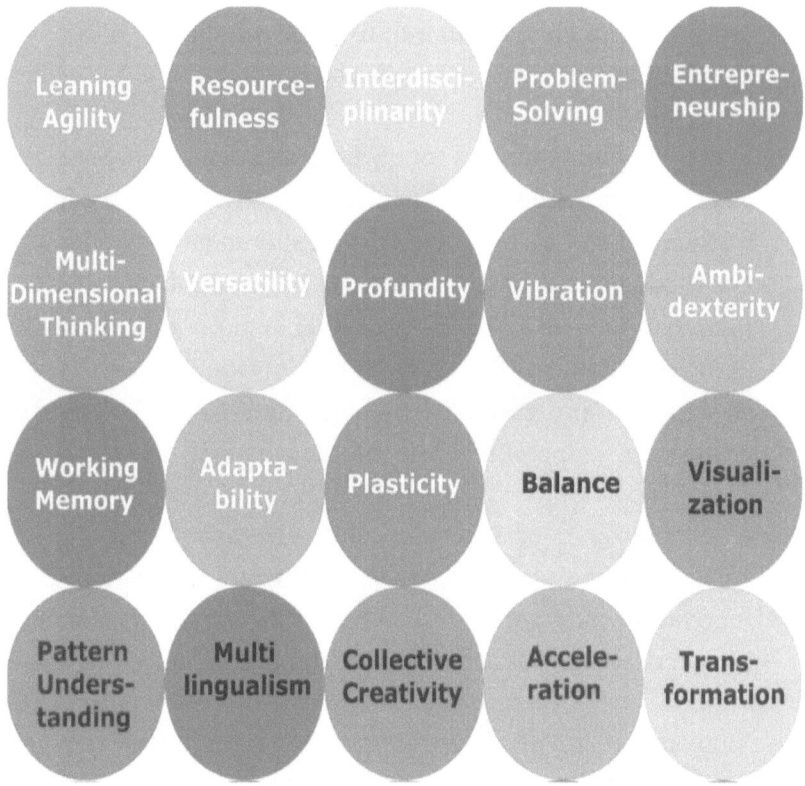

Figure 4 Knowledge and Capability Ingredients

Creativity has just become indispensable. Creativity is a precursor to knowledge in many ways. It couldn't be truer in the digital era. On one hand, the fresh knowledge can be captured from the abundance of information; on the other hand, it doesn't take long for that knowledge to become a commodity once the market is exposed to it. Curiosity stimulates a need to gain knowledge and knowledge is not just book knowledge, but intuitive knowledge feeds the imagination.

There is a philosophical connection between knowledge and creativity. Knowledge is path-dependent. This means that to discover an opportunity, you should have previous knowledge in the field to be able to get recognized. Imagination is also needed to be able to apply this previous knowledge to the different context. Nowadays creativity is an important professional capability, and the multitude of professional capabilities can enforce creativity as well.

At present days, we cannot separate knowledge and creativity if we want to stay competitive on the market. Innovation can happen everywhere; it is our gift as humans; a great deal of what defines us as humans actually.

Innovation is about progress whether it's about new products, services, solutions, new sounds and music, new ways of reading and publishing, new ways of educating future of generations, etc. And the only sustainable competitive advantage is the ability to think different, grow and prosper by continually: LEARNING, INNOVATING, ADAPTING, and EVOLVING.

41

Learning Agility

A learning mind has more dots to connect for sparking innovation.

Learning is a process and everyone has an enormous capacity to learn. Limitations on learning are barriers invented by humans. Learning is multidimensional, dynamic, interactive and integrated. The mind with learning agility likes to experiment and comfortable with change, it can move out of their comfort zone, take risks, and learn from mistakes. It's an important element to spark creativity.

It's important to make connections between pieces of knowledge. When these connections are structured in a meaningful way, we are better at retrieving and applying knowledge effectively and powerfully; or connecting the dots to spark the fresh ideas or to create the new knowledge.

Learning agility means to learn, de-learn and re-learn all the times; and then apply those lessons to succeed in new situations. The mind with learning agility likes to experiment and comfortable with change, it can move out of their comfort zone, take risks, and learn from mistakes. It's an important element to spark creativity.

Learning agility is related to many things such as flexibility, changeability, robustness, sensitivity, comprehensiveness, speed, responsiveness, etc. That is, the multidimensional competencies to formulate creative (unconventional) alternatives or solutions to resolve problems, to show versatility and flexibility in response to unpredictable or unanticipated circumstances.

The **RULEs** to build learning ability: Think outside the box, go against the grain. At times throw away conventional means and try something radically new, and have overall multifaceted resourcefulness.

42

Resourcefulness

Innovators are pioneers, great problem-solvers, and creators of a better context.

Creativity is essentially anchored on the individual's overall multifaceted resourcefulness. That is, the multidimensional (including introspection) competencies to formulate creative, the unconventional alternatives or solutions to resolve problems, to show versatility and flexibility in response to unpredictable or unanticipated circumstances.

With the overwhelming information in the business and our society, it is more crucial to be resourceful, because the static knowledge can be outdated shortly, and often you need to continue to hunt for the latest information for learning and relearning for creativity, decision-making, and problem-solving.

Being resourceful or knowledgeable doesn't necessarily mean you need always to be an expert in a field, but to have some experience on this. It is also true that sometimes if you have too much knowledge on a topic, you will be bounded by this knowledge, hampering being more imaginative about other things. The resourceful people are not those that remember every detail but those that know where to look for knowledge. To be resourceful and objective, you need to always listen to the "two sides of story" or search for contrary viewpoints (if having any) to gaining in-depth understanding and inspire creativity.

The RULEs to be resourceful: Digital professionals need to be intellectually curious, resourceful and learning agile. It's a very powerful confirmation of your present thinking and makes you more resourceful to shape new thinking via exploring the new adventure.

43

Interdisciplinarity

Creativity is a function of imagination, interdisciplinary knowledge, collaboration, and evaluation.

The original germ of a creative idea is often, if not always arrived at through the interaction of ideas from different domains of thought, knowledge, and experience. At present days, we cannot separate knowledge and creativity if we want to stay competitive on the market.

There are both "sensible" knowledge - experience and "intellectual" knowledge -not depending upon experience but in abstract and more "sophisticated" workings. We have a range of different disciplines and qualifications coupled with experiences and ideas, understand the biology and chemistry of the brain, use chemical models, what outside the box should we be thinking of.

Interdisciplinarity is increasingly viewed as a necessary ingredient in spurring creativity. Interdisciplinary simply means to combine knowledge in a new way of gaining in-depth understanding about the complex things today. Creativity starts with a knowledge base, and then openness to new experience or detecting thing you didn't know or applying knowledge from other domains to a new one, results in more creativity in the new domain.

A creative mind desperately needs to absorb the new knowledge cross-disciplinary boundary in order to ponder the creation of the new insight. Not only connect the dots via your own experience but also learn from someone else's experiences, to get more dots for connecting.

The **RULEs** to leverage knowledge for fueling creativity: Keep growth mind, learn from

every experience, but also learn to unlearn the experiences. While imagination helps us expand our idea, knowledge helps us refine our idea to what is economically feasible.

44

Problem-solving

Fundamentally, innovation is to solve old or emergent problems creatively.

Creativity is a solution to a problem. Creativity is to find better ways to do things. Creativity is the discovery of what has not yet been seen nor manifested. Creativity is as much defined by the problem as by the capacity of the individual to connect things to resolve that problem in new and sometimes unexpected ways.

When you encounter a tough problem, you need to use a creative way. Innovation is all about the madness of solving problems and doing things in the newer way. There is as much creative thinking that goes into problem identification as solution finding. Often times, people have a tendency to try to fix a symptom which results from the actual cause of the problem. When they do this, they throw good money after bad. They allow problems to grow under the surface, out of sight, out of mind, until it's too late.

Therefore, it's important to first frame the problems. Creativity is the ability to both frame the questions and solve (or attempt to) problems, framing the right problem is equally or even more important than solving it; it is important to applying creativity in a recursive way to the creative process for both problem identification and problem-solving, Thus, it is a mental process which results in an action that tests a possible solution. Things either work or they do not. That action is creativity.

Both creative and critical thinkers live out of the box, ask open questions to collect relevant information, and think alternatives. You seek for inventions, new designs, creative problem-solving. It drives innovation. In the business world, at least, you can't always wait for the "best" decision to emerge. Creative problem-solving starts with creative communication sets alternative choices, and then you have to make best decisions you can, based on connecting unusual dots, identifying and prioritizing alternative solutions.

The **RULEs** for problem-solving: Creativity is not a "thing," it's a process that happens as a proactive mental activity to a problem. Collective wisdom is often the secret source for creative problem-solving. Co-create alternative visions and dream into existence of new solutions, these are the capacities of humans who are not trapped in 'the same level of thinking' as others or even former personification of 'selves.'

45

Entrepreneurship

Creativity is the "DNA" of entrepreneurs.

Creativity, innovation, and entrepreneurship are often interlinked words. An entrepreneur's mind revolves around new ideas and innovation. Creativity is one of the most crucial traits to be a great entrepreneur.

Entrepreneurship is "about" creating something which did not previously exist. These are both acts of imaginative transformation, of moving beyond anything the mind of the creator can conceive of into a reality that others can perceive and touch and interact with. There are more similarities than differences between those who work as artists and entrepreneurs. Art is most usually seen by artists themselves as being principally about the act of creation; of bringing into existence something which did not previously exist.

Creativity is the "DNA" of entrepreneurs. Entrepreneurs usually dislike the status quo. To become creative, one would have to break down some old rules. After breaking the outdated rules, you are "outside the box." Thinking outside the box is all about "rule breaking"; the more "unruly" you are, the more creative you are. However, being "unruly" incurs risk, you need to set the updated rules for managing the innovation and mitigating the risks, just like shaping the new box to stay focus and achieve the value of creativity.

All of us humans are time-variant expressions across a spectrum of possibility and capability. Entrepreneurship is the creative adventure in search of possibility and builds on capability. None of us stays "the same" from one moment to the next, when the mind flows, your life flows as well- all on a constantly varying scale. Much the same applies to each and every one of us.

The RULEs to practice entrepreneurship:

Entrepreneurship is also about choices. Sometimes there is no "one" answer: there are some or many. That is why what is first of all needed is to advocate entrepreneurship and embrace the collective wisdom. An entrepreneur may not have all the domain knowledge that required transforming an idea into a product, but he or she is able to coordinate the resources from the different knowledge domain required to transform the idea into a product and market.

46

Multidimensional Thinking Capability

Creativity is a higher level of thinking because it often imposes a higher cognitive load as you think "harder" via different thought processes.

Creativity is often analogized as "Out-of-the-Box" thinking; sometimes it is misunderstood as less thinking or gut feeling. In fact, creativity is a complex, multidimensional thought process. Creativity has many dimensions, with multifaceted truth and myth, manifold knowledge and incredible imagination.

Creativity is not just about "out-of-the-box" thinking, to be creative, you need to re-frame the new box thinking. First, you need to embrace the unknown - think outside the box. Second, you need to challenge the knowing (the old box). Third, you can create a bigger box full of new-known. When you are on a higher plane of thinking, you are not confined by the wall, or limited by the hierarchy.

Creativity is a higher level of thinking because it often imposes a higher cognitive load as you think "harder" via different thought processes such as association, perspective shifting, divergent thinking, critical thinking or the conscious-subconscious continuum. Creativity is a flow, an abstract, an imagination and an association -the unusual dots connections. Creativity happens in both unconscious and conscious level. It is a whole brain comprehension.

The **RULEs** for building multidimensional thinking capability: Thinking things differently and making imagination roll into reality is creativity. Digital is the era of innovation; the digital mindset has multidimensional thinking capability and unconventional wisdom via critical thinking, creative thinking, and independent thinking, etc.

47

Versatility

Creative people are optimistic realists to discover versatility.

Creative people embody vitality, will, imagination, hope, and sense of energy. Creativity is about the new box thinking. It takes versatility to shape new, new box, especially noted for transforming old mental maps or paradigms and creating strategies that are "outside the box" of conventional thought. They embody a balance of right brain and left brain thinking, and build a full set of capabilities.

Developing versatility includes a personal action navigated by the habit and the changeability to moving out of a comfort zone leads to the creation of a new comfort zone which in turn will require you to move out "of" it again. This continuous moving "out" of your comfort zone is complemented by the cycle of self-development. "Self-direct" learning is the ability to keep building the new and nonlinear skills and shaping multi-layer, recombinant capabilities for problem-solving and innovation.

Out of this self-development of versatility comes a beautiful thing, the freedom of choice. Once being mindful of the ability to choose, and not being bantered about by habitual emotions and reactive thoughts, the ability to integrate multiple skills to the new abilities, and become more innovative via connecting the unusual dots and transcend interdisciplinary knowledge.

The **RULEs** *to build versatility*: Your potential is unleashed and creativity gets spurred when you find your inner strength. Our brains are working at full speed when it's time for changes; and when you get to a crossroad, your inner strength will bring you perception, persistence, and performance towards the path you take.

48

Profundity

Back to the root of the word "profundity," it means insightful and understanding.

Profundity in understanding things stimulates creativity. A profound mind is like a big ocean, deep, but also open. On one hand, it can leverage multiple thinking processes in spurring creativity and dealing with varying situations wisely. On the other side, creative thinking also plays an instrumental role in developing a greater understanding self, others, and the world, or in short, profundity.

However, there are far too many who do not fully harness their creative ability when it comes down to defining and in some cases refining their own thought process. Creativity helps see problems in multiple dimensions and solve them with passion and innovation.

Climbing Knowledge-Insight-Wisdom pyramid is an important step in gaining profundity. It's not just about knowing, but in-depth understanding; it requires a person's ability to grasp or comprehend information, too often assumptions and prejudices get in the way of understanding. It is the responsibility of individuals to examine themselves and to make sure they are open to true understanding.

Ultimately, creative thinking requires a profound degree of intrapersonal independence and there are far too many people who stand as too intimidated and fearful of harnessing an independent platform in fear of not being good enough in the eyes of others. If we do not direct gradual strides toward its attainment, then we will never know what its substance can do for the potential of our livelihoods.

The **RULEs** *to advocate profundity*: The digital ecosystem is dynamic with velocity, it's important to filling cognitive gaps and sparking the fountain of collective creativity via profound thoughts and inclusive culture.

49

Vibration

Creativity in and of itself is a type of energy vibration.

Creativity is the innate process to create novel ideas. What we call "the mind" is actually referring to the conglomeration of little energy impulses we call "thoughts." Because we experience something called "thoughts," the thoughts piled upon the thought and forms what's being called mind. The brain is the biological organ representing the center of the nervous system. And the mind is the brain sum of cognitive faculties: thinking, judgment, memory, etc.

The mind is the conscious energy that engulfs the brain; it works through the brain. The mind has to do with the flow of energy, like software, thinking is only a small aspect of consciousness. And the mind would be more between people, in their interaction. If the mind is a characteristic of living creatures, then it is highly related to what makes a living creature to be creative.

The higher the frequency of the vibration, the more positive energy flows out to spark creativity. Creative people sense, feel, read, imagine and intuit possibilities in the digital paradigm shift. While we each have the enormous creative capacity, our willingness to exercise and express it becomes more complicated. We are all complex beings with highs and lows of vibration and all these feelings are "worthy" of being expressed.

The **RULEs** to create vibration: Accessing and keeping the creative energy flow or vibrated is the source of inspiration, imagination and ideation, intelligence, and a high level of the thinking process. Self-motivation is a significant component in the expression of creativity. If someone has the desire to be curious and involved in a situation, their innate creativity will push them along to a limited extent. In this energy all things are possible.

50

Ambidexterity

To put simply, ambidexterity is the capability to balance.

Generally speaking, ambidexterity means an individual can adapt to use both left hand and right hand smoothly. From a creativity perspective, an ambidextrous individual is a person who can leverage multiple thought processes to think differently; and an "ambidextrous organization" is an organization that can handle innovation streams for different purposes with different time frames and through different methodologies.

To be creative, to re-frame, you need to do two things. First, you need to embrace the unknown (think outside the box). Second, you need to challenge the known (probe the paradoxes). Put another way, you need to both step up a level (n+1) and drill down a level (n-1), to think or observe with ambidexterity. To put simply, ambidexterity is the capability to balance. Creativity needs a balance of divergent and convergent thinking, simplicity and complexity thinking, intuition and critical thinking, etc.

Thinking creatively = creating a new box that could be used for thinking inside the new box, but out of the old box for one or more class of problems. The infamous "box" can have many sides. It may be a geodesic shaped box with many faces. Fundamentally, the "box" is the set of "rules" you are abiding by at any moment in time. There are likely multiple "boxes" that you try to stay within. Working within multiple sets would create an "intersection of sets," which can cultivate ambidexterity, stimulate new ideas and spur creativity.

The RULEs to be ambidextrous: The

ambidexterity - a good combination of complexity thinking and simplicity thinking are important to fuel digital creativity because the work is different from what it was in the past, it is easy to believe that it is more complex. The complexity thinking enables you to think the problems more systematically and solve them more holistically; and simplicity thinking continues to optimize your thought process, to make the solution simple but not simpler, smart but also elegant.

51

Working Memory

The veins, vessels, and synapses of the brain are like a computer with memory, able to download and process information accordingly.

The human brain is perhaps one of the most mysterious things in the world. The concept of brain emulation has a colorful history, roughly 85 billion individual neurons make up the human brain, each one connects to as many as 10, 000 others via axons and dendrites. All of the mind's requests are then processed, implemented, and interfaced by the brain.

The veins, vessels, and synapses of the brain are like a computer with memory, able to download and process information accordingly. It's the sum of those brain signals that encode information and enable the brain to process, associate and execute commands. And many neuroscientists believe the essence of which we are, the memory, the personality, the emotion, the thinking process, and even the consciousness- lies in those brain patterns. To put simply you are what you think.

Creativity makes the human mind still much superior to computers, even though we often lose the calculation game to the computers today. Creativity is a complex neuro-psycho-philosophical phenomenon which is difficult to define literally. Fundamentally it involves the ability to understand and express novel orderly relationships. The creative process involves four stages - preparation, incubation, illumination and verification.

A high level of general intelligence, domain specific knowledge, and special skills via quality memory capacity are necessary prerequisites to cultivate creativity. Associated with such pre-requisites, the process of creative innovation (incubation and illumination stages) necessitates the need for an ability of divergent thinking, a novelty-seeking behavior, some degree of suppression of latent inhibition and a subtle degree of frontal dysfunction.

The RULEs to improve memory capacity:

Working memory does play a role in boosting creativity. The collective sensation is one's perspective, experience, memory, imagination, perception. Modern technologies make it easier for neurologists to look inside the brain and understand how it is functioning and growing. It is even in a tipping point where they can actually see inter-neural connections forming and firing to stimulate creativity.

52

Adaptability

Adaptability enforces creativity, and creativity is adaptability.

Adaptability is to be understood as the ability of a person or system to adapt self efficiently and fast to changed circumstances. Each person has a different level of knowledge (the consciousness about a problem) and adaptability to react to environmental changes, with behaviors that are strictly linked to the information they have and with the way other people share and collaborate with them. Creativity is adaptability, and adaptability further enforces creativity.

Digital is about changes; closer to reality is that 'change' is continuously happening in such a dynamic environment. Nature and human societies are a nonlinear 'complex adaptive system' inhabiting interacting agents that adapt to each other and their environment. However, People normally 'close' the boundaries of the system, so that less energy is transferred and, therefore, the fewer changes happen in the system. We all try to 'close' the system, so to say, to reduce its complexity, but also stifle creativity. The adaptive attitude is to manage complexity via agility enhancement, to keep creativity flow, and the mind flow.

We need a complete picture of the environment to which the brain is adapting to - to figure out what is going on within the brain. It is not only something in an environment fostering connectivity within our brains. The connectivity within our brains also shapes our environment.

Through creativity (imagining, testing the hypothesis, failing, entreating, improving), the new knowledge is developed. If we do all these things well, then people and the organizations we inhabit adapt to the ever changing environment and evolve in an ideal world to improved levels of form, function, and prosperity. And, in this, an individual could develop a new connectivity, fostering similar connectivity in many other brains.

The **RULEs** to be adaptable: Digital attitude is about adaptability - being experimental and changeable. As an individual, you definitely have to adapt to change, learn new skills, and are genuinely eager to contribute in the new environment to the new digital realities.

53

Plasticity

Neuroplasticity is the key to unlocking ultimate creativity.

Neu-ro-plas-tic-ity refers to the life-long capac-ity of the brain to change and rewire itself in response to the stim-u-la-tion of learn-ing and expe-ri-ence. Because openness to new knowledge and experience is significantly important to creativity, our brain plasticity is the higher-order factors that can subsume openness.

Brain plasticity, also known as neuroplasticity, is a term that refers to the brain's ability to change and adapt as a result of openness to experience. We can "build" new neural pathways, increase the overall density of the "neural map" and synapses, etc., and neu-ro-ge-n-e-sis is the abil-ity to cre-ate new neu-rons and con-nec-tions between neu-rons through-out a life-time to develop cognitive abilities, including creativity.

The brain is an amazing organ; the neurons can develop new dendrites to rewire itself if it needs to. The brain "emerges from a process." And actually, all physiology emerges from that process. Brain plasticity is a reflection of the intrinsic flexibility 'of that process,' to increase thinking capacities and ignite creativity.

The RULEs to improve plasticity:

Neuroplasticity is the key to unlocking ultimate creativity. Keep using your brain wisely, and keep learning as the lifetime habit. It means your brain can not only grow but also change when you continue to use it actively; it becomes more proactively connecting the dots and developing your creativity.

54

Balance

Creativity needs encouragement as the spirit of food, and conflict to spark it.

Creativity is essentially anchored on the individual's multidimensional thinking ability to strike the right balance and the overall multifaceted resourcefulness, with distinctive competencies to formulate creative alternatives or solutions to resolve problems, to show versatility and agility in response to unpredictable or unanticipated circumstances.

Creativity exists between the two contradictory human drives of needing others and needing to establish one's own identity. It's about balance. To balance well, it's all about being creative, to think cross-boxes, and to overcome extreme thinking and silo mentality.

On the one hand, you need to feel part of a group, at which time it is your similarity with others that is salient. On the other hand, you need to establish your own identity and uniqueness, when it is our difference from others that is salient. This is happening like a time spiral whereby you leave the comfort of the group to be creative, and then return to it to fulfill the group needs, and have others recognize the fruits of your creativity.

Engaging in creativity inevitably creates tension, conflict, and emotionally charged debates and disagreements because we need both control and predictability, creativity and change, the balance of opposite forces to reach the creative tension, whether you like it or not, because it gives uncertainty and insecurity with new and change.

The **RULEs** to cultivate creativity via

<u>BALANCE</u>: Creativity loves the challenge, the courage to see the new; creativity is fresh and new every time. It does not fear. It has that emotional or affective strength to trust the process of creativity. Creativity needs encouragement as the spirit of food, and conflict to spark it up. Conflict makes the mind think differently leading to creativity. The combination of good chemical balance is reinforced, because it does not go for repeating due to helplessness but due to fun and the joy of life.

55

Visualization

The true conflict in innovation is self-imposed by trying to make our "visions" reality.

Creating a visualization of what you want to accomplish can be a powerful practice to spur creativity. A creative person is effective in manifesting his or her vision because she/he creates specific, achievable goals, initiates action and enlists the participation of others. The vision if understood in the perspective of creativity becomes a reality achievable and a comprehensible dream beyond words.

From a neurological perspective, some studies show that creative and methodical solvers exhibit different activities in areas of the brain that process visual information. The patterns of "alpha" and "beta" brainwaves in creative solvers were consistent with diffuse rather than focused visual attention. This may allow creative individuals to broadly sample the environment for experiences that can trigger remote associations to produce an "Aha Moment."

There are times when we feel driven by forces that we don't understand. So visualization helps bring awareness to these unconscious motivations. Just as we find energy is released from one steady state to another, we find innovation from our outer realities attempts to change to the steady state of our inner self. This energy is called innovation. The conflict can come from an internal conflict or a conflict with the outside world. The true conflict in innovation is self-imposed by trying to make our "visions" reality. The most difficult part is to transform the conflict from within to a productive life cycle. This is about understanding the wholeness.

The **RULEs** to enforce creativity via visualization: Learn to visualize for inspiring creativity, and make imagination rolling into reality. Nowadays there is a digital convenience of being innovative. Lots of tools are available to help us think visually, differently and communicate effectively, assess problems and come to solutions in novel ways. There is possible development of new brain imaging techniques for assessing the potential of creative thought, and for assessing the effectiveness of visualization methods for training individuals to think creatively.

56

Pattern Understanding

Pattern understanding is the type of problem-solving thinking.

Pattern thinking and perception are critical ingredients of creativity. Pattern thinking is the type of problem-solving thinking skill. If you look at patterns, you will find that they are containers for describing relationships because that is what gives them their sense. They are defined as "solutions of problems in a context" with a body of "descriptions of forces."

What could be in stronger relationship to us than something that solves a problem for us? Pattern Thinking, therefore, is more crucial in the complex digital world. Nature and human societies are a nonlinear 'complex adaptive system' with inhabiting interacting elements that adapt to each other and their environment. It is a nonlinear, dynamic and open system in a thermodynamic sense. Unlike closed equilibrium system, it hence spontaneously self-organizes; generates patterns, structures, and complexity; and above all, creates novelty over time.

People's brains function differently and have different tendencies, and that also applies to seeing patterns versus seeing a part in isolation. However, we all have some bias and subjective perception. Our tendency to get attached to the poor choices, an outcome that is the result of another set of biased cognitive processes leading to more problems, when uncertainty, ambiguity, and complexity are all today's digital normality. We 'know' a lot of 'things,' we also 'know' that the multitude of these 'things' is not necessarily 'just true,' they might be potentially true, potentially partially true, potentially possibly true. We also 'have knowledge' about 'things' where we do not necessarily 'know' about what is 'true' but instead of 'what is not true.' Pattern Thinking does help us solve such a jigsaw puzzle creatively.

Furthermore, the language, culture do impact people's pattern understanding ability, or how overall people thinking. Some cultures appear to have more people who look at the whole rather than the parts. The question is, would this be due to cultural influences, education, or brain functionality/ tendencies that are common to the people born in that cultural setting?

The **RULEs** of pattern understanding: Pattern thinking is a type of creative thinking because it requires you to keep your eyes open and keep your mind out of the box in order to shape the bigger box and actively seek out new ideas wherever you can discover them. So, it is a hybrid thinking to combine design thinking, system thinking, architect thinking and visual thinking for solving complex problems or capturing deep insight.

57

Multilingualism

A multi-linguistic mindset is multi-faceted to think from a different angle.

Languages have a huge impact on the way the brain organizes itself to think and express. Language is an art in its own right. Languages have so many different intricacies and facets, which make it difficult to define which aspect is actually the differential aspect that influences thought or creativity. The language itself is the best creative thing ever happened to the human society.

A multi-linguistic mindset can improve one's cognitive skills including creativity. Speaking more languages rather than just one has obvious practical benefits in an increasingly globalized world. But in recent years, scientists have begun to show that the advantages of multilingualism are even more fundamental than being able to converse with a wider range of people. Being multilingual can have a profound effect on your brain, improving cognitive skills not related to language and is proven to sharpen the brain, memory, to think creatively and strategically and on the spot.

A multi-linguistic mindset nourishes curiosity and cultivates creativity. Learning multiple languages provides the important nourishment for understanding different cultures and societies at a level that is not possible to reach otherwise. It provides the insight on why people are what they are and what makes them tick formed through a diversity of cultures and nuances. This is something which cannot be taught but only gained through daily exposure.

The **RULES** to practice multi-linguistic creativity: A multi-linguistic mindset is more inclusive of the diverse point of view. The more languages you learn one at a time, the easier, the more you discover different logics and thought processes and improve creativity via thinking from various points of views. As you learn both logic and synthesis from those language configurations, it can also be easier for you to think out of the old box.

58

Collective Creativity

While the individual contributions provide the "building block" of creativity, it is the collective consensus on what to do with them that is exciting.

Being creative is the kind to "think outside the box" for ideas and solutions. But the creative spark does not always originate solely in the individual. In that manner, you could say there is more collective creativity happening everywhere than many realize because it is really hard for some people to see outside of their own box.

The exercise of blending people's problem-solving abilities to produce the desired outcome is a worthwhile thing to do. It is not just a mere accumulation of the creative inputs of those involved. It is more than that. It has its own dynamic that is in a state of constant flux. It builds up a momentum that draws creative contributions from the participants that they did not previously conceive or understood they were capable of.

However, the group of people does not always make creativity blossom. You can get a diverse group of people together in one room and still not have "creativity" if the participating individuals are not particularly creative. What matters is how creative are the individuals.

Creativity can manifest in a collective environment. While the individual contributions provide the 'building block" of creativity, it is the collective consensus on what to do with them that is exciting, by manifesting creativity from an individual endeavor to a team activity and a collective effort, the horizon of creativity is expanded, it converges with the concept of innovation that is the management discipline to transform innate ideas and achieve its business value.

The RULEs for amplifying collective creativity: The collective creativity depends on varying factors because the team perhaps has different intents (destructive vs. constructive), different processes (enforcement vs. collaboration), different participants (compliant vs. creative), different outcomes (disharmony vs. harmony) and different philosophies (selflessness vs. selfishness).

59

Acceleration

Digital professionals with accelerated mind continue to learn and develop creativity and recombinant professional capabilities.

People have different mindset and attitude to adapt to changes and influence surroundings. Fixed mindset has the assumption that their abilities were innate and not subject to change; while accelerated or growth mind refers to those who solve problems or target the goals with growth mind, with the belief that their ability level is nothing more than a snapshot in time and eminently changeable as they continue to learn and develop creativity and recombinant professional capabilities.

Fixed mindset sticks to the old way to do things while accelerated and growth mind enjoys new thinking. In the industrial era, fixed mindset is OK to survive as the business and the world are slow to change; however, at today's Digital Era, knowledge is only a click away, what we need is not just a faster speed, but a hyper-connected ecosystem, with growth mindsets and the spirit of creativity. The growth mind is a strategic imperative to adapt to changes, and accelerated mind is needed to match the digital speed.

The **RULEs** *for acceleration.* Digital professionals with an accelerated mind can stay focus, set priority and discipline, enforce strengths and unleash their creativity potential. These innovators have what we call the accelerated mind which is authentic, audacious, adaptive, and aggressive when necessary.

60

Transformation

A transformation often needs to break down the outdated rules that make "creativity" a unique trait.

Innovation is the change. Change is a basic human ability to inspire self and others to look beyond limitations, keep creativity flow, and make a continuous journey of improvement.

Change is the very nature of the digital era. Transformation is the leapfrogging change. A transformation has long-range perspective and focuses on goals of innovation. You cannot make the omelet without breaking a few eggs. A transformation often needs to break down the outdated rules that make "creativity" a unique trait for digital professionals today.

Changing the game is the mindset. In addition to the set point changing, transformation requires first shifting mindsets, and then, building new nonlinear skills and integral capabilities including creativity, reinforcing and embedding new practices/reflexes. From being curious to creative to critical, the emphasis of digital transformation should be put new ways to improve surrounding and the world. The digital philosophy comes from a worldview that looks at the world as one. It's a holistic view that sees the world as interconnected, interdependent, and integrated. It means to understand human's difference and pursue creativity and uniqueness.

Change may be mechanical, but the transformation is radical and innovative. For what can be called "implement-table innovation." The term transformational change, when applied to an organization, carries with a sense of "evolution" which means, a renewed understanding of the future of business; what're the disruptive trends; how your organization catalyzes the positive and progressive changes and how much better one can do to leverage creativity and lead a seamless transformation.

The RULEs to drive transformational innovation: At the individual level, creativity is the

personal brand and needs to be a healthy habit, or even not so bad addiction. At the organizational level, innovation should become a digital lifestyle of a company. Transformational innovation won't take place if their core tendencies in the business life cycle aren't identified and overcome.

Chapter 4 Creative Activity Ingredients

Creativity is like a muscle; you must exercise it daily or it atrophies.

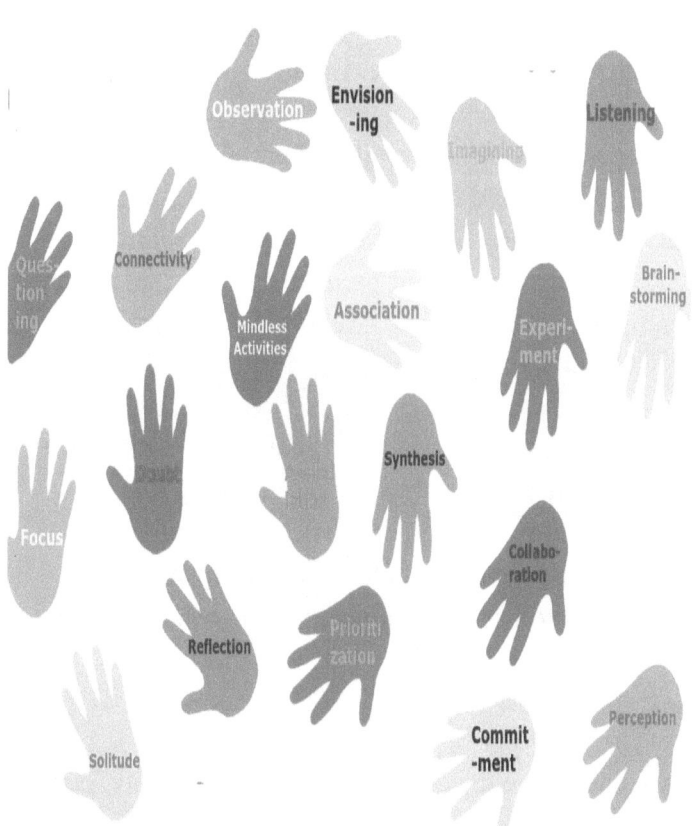

Figure 5 Creative Activity Ingredients

Digital knowledge workforce has high creativity potential. Creativity is like a muscle; you must exercise it daily or it atrophies. Today's digital professionals are innovative workers, hard workers, knowledge workers and intelligent workers, who are exploring, innovating and evolving in bringing new digital paradigms.

Unleashing creativity is a journey and flexing creativity muscle is a continuous practice. Creative people tend to be non-conformists, or, at least, appear to be, however, that is just the way they think, not really intentional. Creative people judge the world for themselves and they are skeptical of but open with outside opinions. Creative people define and create their own convention that they live by in comparison to everyone else who just accept or inherit their convention to live by.

Creative people bring in bright, original and creative ideas, they have an infectious enthusiasm for making things better. They continually and constructively challenge the status quo and have positive ideas for improvement. They consistently act to improve things in their own role or team, and they actively support and adapt well to changes proposed by others.

While we each have the enormous creative capacity, our willingness to exercise and express it becomes more complicated. We are all complex beings with highs and lows and all these feelings are "worthy" of being expressed. If someone has the desire to be curious and involved in a situation, their innate creativity will push them along. Creative people are inspired to think and work nearly every day on creating, they are not waiting for the "Aha" moment, but proactively stimulating the new energy with the fountain of creativity. After all, we all find new ways to make our work "easier," more rewarding, better for ourselves, our customers, and our society.

61

Observation

Observation is a critical activity in the innovation process to understand the context of an issue from a human perspective.

Observation is an important ingredient of creativity, also a crucial stage in innovation. It is the state of being mindful and conscious about the surrounding. There are three stages of "Observation." First, the best observations come from staying still and trying to understand what you're observing is all about. So staying a novice of some sort, keep fresh eyes, with the beginner's mind. Then try to do the very things you've been observing because it will bring much more insights when you try to fiddle with it.

Secondly, observation is not just about seeing, but understanding; what you see depends very much on what you are familiar with and on the parading - there is no such thing as pure data, it's contextual, and it's a personal story. Creative observation means that you can see things from different angles, see above, underneath, and around the corner, to capture the new insight or ignite creativity.

Thirdly, like many things we do, observation needs a goal, and observers need a purpose. Cognitive science confirms that what you see depends very much on your goals and on what you concentrate on given the limited amount of working memory available. Quality observation brings unique perception and stimulates creativity.

Observation is always the first step of any meaningful discovery journey, either for practicing innovation or decision making; it brings your life to the new height for being a thoughtful human being or growing you into an empathetic and innovative leader to drive digital transformation.

The **RULEs** for observation: Observe, observe, observe more, through your cool head and sharp eyes, and engage your five senses, to watch, to hear, to touch, to feel and to taste. Experience, adaptability, flexibility, synthesis, and concentration are all crucial characteristics to decide the quality of observation.

62

Envisioning

Creative expanding cannot happen without vision.

Envisioning is the imagination's inner screen lighting up in the context of where the imagination grows. To envision is the focus coming in contact with the natural deployment, grown from the whole envisioning atmosphere you soak in daily life.

A clear vision is not clouded and distorted by rosy colored glasses or narrow-minded perspectives. A clear vision is circular, not tunnel; multi-dimensional, not single lenses; and colorful, not black and white. It should be vivid enough to tell the story and positive enough to overcome barriers; it touches the hearts and minds; it inspires creativity and drives actions.

A clear vision can boost creativity and sustain innovation. Envisioning should have a direction which sets in clarity - setting a vision that isn't high enough doesn't challenge the group of people to excel. But establishing a vision that is based on unrealistic expectations will either discount the value of even creating the vision or disenfranchise stakeholders. Vision should be attainable; however, the vision shouldn't be a fixed target. It should be stable enough to make it worthwhile to make a concerted effort to attain it and dynamic enough to be able to react to any change in direction or context.

The **RULEs** to envision: Creative expanding cannot happen without vision. We have no choice but to participate in our vision. Being conscious and becoming self-aware, is a choice we actively make in each moment. A vision should be attainable subject to current times and its ability to adapt to changing times; vision is the destination, creativity is the tail wind, and innovation is the part of a strategy to get there.

63

Imagining

Imagination is like virtual creativity, formless and intangible.

Imagination is the fuel for the "Creativity Engine." Creativity is an actual project or idea carried out in a tangible way that offers or shows something new or imagined. No imagination, the engine will not run. Imagination is conscious thinking in images. It is the thinking we are aware of. Conscious thinking or imagination is a precursor to expression.

Creativity brings into the form that reflects the individuality and uniqueness. Imagination can entertain the seemingly impossible, given the right resources of knowledge, experience, and talent; a bridge may be created between the current 'impossible' to a whole new 'possible.' This is probably our story from the first cave paintings to where we are at now, an evolutionary two-step between the imagination and creativity.

Creativity is part imagination and part knowledge. Creativity is sparked by an implicit rather than explicit underbelly of knowledge. Imagination is the seed to grow innovation. Imagination is the ability to expand the boundaries of knowledge and capture insight. That creativity in the human sense is not due to connecting of two shallow pools of knowledge, but the ability to make deep connections and build on those connections to generate novel ideas.

Imagination inspires your learning attitude as well because often imagination blooms at the beginners' mind; they enjoy experimenting and discovering; there's no rule to limit their imagination. Why being creative is not just about "knowledgeable"? Because they are often at the edge of things and able to expand the boundaries of knowledge.

The **RULEs** for imagining: Thinking things differently and making imagination roll into reality is creativity. An open mind leads to imagination, imagination leads to discovery, discovery leads to innovation, and innovation leads to technology advancement and societal progression.

64

Listening

Listening is an important skill to spark creativity and cultivate empathy.

Creativity is an innate part of being human, and listening is a crucial component in the process of creativity. There are all sorts of listening skills - critical listening to capture information; intuitive listening to touch hearts; selective listening to confirm the point of views; precision listening to pay attention to details; or empathetic listening to gain understanding, etc. Listening is an important skill to develop creativity. All those valuable listening skills enhance knowledge assimilation and improve continuous adaptability for enabling dots-connecting and stimulating creativity.

Listening "attentively" and actively is the greatest gift we can give to another human being as well. The real beauty is found in the ability to listen from your heart, invite the speaker to explore the answers that lie within their own hearts and minds, with the possibility to unlock creativity with both parties.

However, due to the rush and fast pace of modern life, people interrupt and seek to solve the problem, often before they have heard enough to understand what is being said and whether anything is truly being asked of us beyond just listening. Effective listening goes far deeper than we understand for unlocking creativity.

The **RULES** to listen. Listening is all about connecting as humans, and igniting creativity, whether at work or elsewhere. When we listen and find out the other's purpose, identify and respect, whether we agree with it or not, be non-judgmental, then we can connect, talk about it, discuss it and many times, they will get more insight and will look at it differently and be able to fine tune their own purpose, which they never thought about it in such a way. This is the power of listening to spark creativity.

65

Questioning

The good question is usually open and thought provoking to bring multifaceted perspectives.

Creative people ask questions, usually questions no one else would think of, or initiate the open and bold inquiries such as "Why Not," or "What if." Good questions evoke imagination and great questions inspire creativity. In fact, questioning is one of the important stages (observing, questioning, connecting, networking) for developing creativity.

Creative people are both problem finders and problem solvers and always challenge conventional wisdom by asking questions which often lead to discovering situations others do not see at first. Doesn't the real solution to innovation or creativity begin with inquiry?

Too often, when asking questions, you tend to assume that the people who are answering actually understand your language. Many times, that is not the case and leads to a misalignment between "what you need" vs. "what you get." Therefore, pay more attention to the "lost in translation" symptom, and connect the real dots between inquiries and answers, in order to spark creativity.

Creativity is the "soaring factor." Creativity is the wind. Creativity is the saving grace. We may ask the wrong questions, tell ourselves the wrong answers and creativity gives it all another chance to make it right. The challenge is perhaps that, this can earn you a label of being 'negative,' because you question everything. Thus, it is important to build a culture of creativity and encourage asking learning questions.

The **RULEs** to make inquiries. The good question is usually open and thought provoking. The good question brings multifaceted perspective. Your mind is connecting the dots and your vision become clear - so be sensitive to your intuition and listen to it. Frequently, by deeply observing and relentlessly questioning, the resulting work becomes richer and more evocative for the creative inspiration you come up with. So, keep asking.

66

Connectivity

Creativity is like the light, the reason we see the light because the "switch" is on and the connection is made.

Creativity is about connecting the dots. In life we come across various experiences via exposure to various situations as colorful dots, the more dots we have, the better chance our mind can connect them freely. Connectivity triggers the ignition of the inflammable material leading to a series of effects. The spark of innovation would benefit the mankind when the brainstorming is translating the innovative idea into tangible reality.

A creative mind has such an "AHA" moment, just like the very moment when light bulb switch is on -the transcendence from darkness to brightness. It is not the light, but the process of "clicking or switching" giving rise to "glowing." When the "switch" is on, the connection is made. If we look to the light bulb, as a symbol of idea and creativity. The reason we have seen the light, because the "switch" is on and the connection is made. The "AHA" moment sparks the new beam of innovation light to see the things and the world differently and approach the problems with the new insight and foresight. It could be an "out of the box" thinking or intuition.

A creative mind is just like a light bulb, proactively making dots connections across knowledge domains, experiences, languages, and cultures; the more dots you have, the more hyper-connected your mind turns to be, and the more creative you become, just like a light bulb, you seem to be brighter and lighten up the surrounding as well.

To be creative, you need to be conscious, curious about things that surround you. To be conscious is to be aware and engaged with both the inner world of thought, feeling, choice, and the exterior world of experience and relationship. The interaction between these two parts of our existence is the home of our creativity. It is the grist for our creative mill. It enables to connect seemingly unconnected items to build something new.

The **RULEs** to be highly connected: Digital is about hyperconnectivity. How cleverly you connect your dots by leveraging your experiences and finding a solution to the problems is creativity, it is also an important aspect of digital fluency.

67

Mindless Activities - Sleep, Walk, Stretch, Meditate...

The more mindless the task, the higher probability of subconscious disruption can stimulate creativity.

The "AHA" moment of creativity often comes from the "unexpected moment." One of the things that quite dramatically improve creativity is doing a mindless task, which may go some way to explaining why 'AHA moments' come when you are, for instance, going for a walk.

Our minds have access to both conscious thoughts and at times unconscious thought. It is a conscious mind we call with some unconscious activities of allowing creativity flow. As many creatives or inventors may tell you, ideas tend to come when you stop thinking about the problem. Hence, some seemly "mindless" activities such as walking, stretching, meditation or even sleeping can ignite your creativity and reach the precious "Aha!" moment.

It is not clear whether the task has to be physical (like taking the walk), or whether it could be mental, such as the repetition of the mantra during meditation. Either way, it is clear that creativity, in general, can be enhanced by performing a task, with the subject of the creative effort having nothing to do with the task. It is just leaving things to subconscious thinking. During the repetitive tasks, the subconscious capacity can sometimes produce creative ideas for disparate tasks, though. Subconscious thinking is often quick, and efficient. Using that form of thinking, people perform tasks without being aware of what has been done.

In addition, to be interactively creative within a task is to suppress any automation or disembodiment, to become immersive with it. That is not to say that during this repetitive task that our subconscious capacity cannot or will not produce creative ideas for other related or even disparate tasks. Not at all, in fact, the more mindless the task is, the higher probability of subconscious disruption happens. In fact, the process of 'preloading' the subconscious capacity with a task (requiring a creative solution) and then deliberately distracting the conscious mind is quite common in stimulating creativity.

*The **RULEs** for doing "mindless activities" to stimulate creativity*: Take a walk, or have a good sleep, be "mindless" to stimulate subconsciousness of the brain to boost your creativity. The purposeful manipulation of the stages of 'preparation,' 'incubation,' and 'illumination' is a widespread protocol for creative output among professionals.

68

Association

Context is a chain of associations which stimulate creativity.

Creativity has two parts: The spark of inspiration (1st thought) which plants a new concept in our heads, and then the building of a structure of associations and relationships between that "seed" concept, and the many concepts already stored in our heads. The associations and relationships are what turn the spark into an expressible idea, and if we are lucky a useful idea.

The original germ of a creative idea is often, if not always arrived at through the interaction of ideas from different domains of thought and experience; it is inherently 'illogical,' from a conventional perspective. The initial spark only comes after your brain has toiled with the problem. Your subconscious brain loves creating solutions to problems that plague your conscious brain. Anytime an idea "pops" into your head, you have your subconscious to thank. Very rarely can you power your way through a problem using purely conscious thought.

The process of creativity may not conform to any known logic, as it can wander and be influenced by disparate associations brought up during the act of exploring. We all use our creativity to solve problems for what is creativity about, an ability to seek solutions to problems. There is no guarantee of a correct answer, just an attempt to find one. It's how we learned to walk and talk for example.

The **RULEs** for making the association to stimulate creativity:
We can create the context for the chain of association to stimulate creativity. It's like when you contemplate a work of art. You don't get the whole idea immediately. It has to grow on you, sometimes one piece by the other piece. The implications of its effects reach beyond the visual. It also triggers a chain of associations. You see it in another context, or you might see the influences of another domain colliding with the expected domain to spark creativity.

69

Experiment

Creativity isn't necessarily a paint-by-numbers process, more as a 'connect-the-dots" adventure.

Experiment means to try new things. Creativity is an experiment. Creativity is the mental activities involving imagining, association, and experimenting. Creativity usually, perhaps more often than not, involves some level of discomfort and interdisciplinary transcendence. The problem is that we can't order and classify creativity in the typical worldview.

Creativity is the experimental adventure. Creativity is a synthesis of two qualities: Imagination with which you create new ideas and the concreteness with which you can transform ideas into real work. Play, experiment and explore. Creativity isn't necessarily a paint-by-numbers process, more as a 'connect-the-dots" adventure.

Innovation takes the cycle of observing-questioning-connecting-networking-experimenting. Build an innovation incubator for experimentation. Set criteria and build principles to select the right talent for creativity. Select for empowerment, select for curiosity, select for low ego.

Select the ones who love the clash of ideas, love listening, love being wrong, love learning. Facilitate coaching up, sideways and all around; encourage appreciative inquiry; empower change agents who challenge status quo and thought leaders who break barriers. Select for the diversity of perspective, background, and personality. Provide the environment that hosts and experiments the stream of ideas, make everybody innovative and make the proper rewarding system.

The **RULEs** for experimenting: Innovation comes from the environment in which thinking and experimenting are stimulated. Encourage and reward "creative thinking." Make sure people have some time to do creative thinking. It's very hard to explore "what if?" thoughts if 110% of your time is spent on mundane tasks. Experiment more and do more with innovation.

70

Brainstorming

Many creative minds, just like many light bulbs lit up simultaneously, could lead to brainstorming and breakthrough innovation.

The digital brainstorming is happening in real time with people and plays spontaneous networks of human and business concerns, to co-solve many thorny problems and overcome numerous challenges facing humanity. Brainstorming activates creativity which can be transformed into innovation. The key to brainstorming is not to evaluate your ideas. Just let the ideas flow. There are idea generation techniques (such as brainstorming) in which an idea is followed in several directions to lead to one or more new ideas, which in turn lead to more ideas.

In order to think out-of-the-box and to "silence the noise of the mind," one needs to be involved in a menial task that does not require much of a conscious effort to execute, thus allowing background operations to run such as brainstorming a solution to a problem. At the team level, having brainstorm helps problem identification to avoid "worrying about the wrong thing" symptom. So a few innovation traits include:

-Learn to forget what you have been "educated" in the past.

-Start using the other half brain for a change.

-Learn to trust and follow your gut feeling to capture insight

The root of innovation is basically "an innovative idea" which when shared amidst a group of innovators, just like many light bulbs lit up simultaneously, could lead to brainstorming, fine-tuning, refining and ultimately crystallizing into a realistic plan and implementation. The innovation lies in channelization of employees' ideas on any particular aspect and makes them 'brainstorm' so that there are individual and collective outcomes that can lead to new technologies, solutions, or paths.

The RULEs for brainstorming: Many creative minds, like the firework, shine up the sky. Many creative minds getting together are just like holiday lights lit up, not for decoration, but for inspiration and brainstorming.

71

Focus

Curiosity and a sense of adventure are parts of the creative process, and not necessarily at odds with the word 'focus.'

We have the opportunity to continue learning and being creative. It's about how you can generate a specific energy in yourself to help consciously create the authentic impact you choose. Creativity is a function of knowledge, imagination, and evaluation. However, besides those elements, the most important element is the attitude put to increase the chance of generating creative ideas. Focus provides motivation and demolishes negative emotion.

A combination of conscious and unconscious factors allows us to follow through our initial creative impulse; idea generation process is also the capacity to focus. Focus gains clarity. Clarity increases awareness and awareness taps into new, creative and innovative views of the world. It appears that the evolution of the human will have to come from the ease of ignoring distractions or to become more focused.

Creative people have the great joy of bringing a new idea, concept to the life. These are people who are more focused on "what's next," than "look what I did!" It's all in the attitude and mind to keep creativity flow. Lack of 'FOCUS' is an impediment to creativity. Particularly for most of the people whose natural bent is to perhaps be all over the place. Being focused can harmonize your brainpower with nature energy in stimulating creativity. Whether you focus for a brief period to accomplish one thing or set aside specific times to do specific things, it's the key to success for innovators. *"You cannot depend on your eyes when your imagination is out of focus."* — Mark Twain

Time is the order of moments in which the mind spurs creativity and perceives the changes. Dedicated people focus on thinking, growing or innovating, their energy flows forward and makes a positive influence on the surroundings. Hence, the effective time management boosts creativity.

The RULEs to stay focus. Focus and dedication boost creativity, though sometimes you need to take the "mindless' activities to reach the "Eureka Moment." It makes you creative oriented, mature and generous enough to share insight and wisdom with others. It makes you bold and shed the fear of failure, lethargic tendency and any inability that prevent you from being creative and progressive.

72

Doubt

Without constructive skepticism, without human progress.

Positive doubt or skepticism triggers creativity and leads to better problems-solving and progression. Doubt or skepticism in its constructive manner and reasonable proportion is a positive force of mind. And being creative or innovative is more often than not path-breaking, thereby effecting bifurcation point in human history.

In fact, the right dose of skepticism is the great ingredient to developing creativity. Without it, you won't make inquiry; without questioning, you won't explore the new possibilities and practice creativity. Without a doubt, the world will stand still, no progress is being made. Societies across the world put emphasis on conventional wisdom as the quintessential value for life. This is because; societies obstinately discourage change and conserve ideas and doctrines for maintaining social order and functionality. Free thinkers normally do not fall in line with the dogmatic and obsolete social systems. They pose threat and menace to the complacency of the common person's perception of life and conventional wisdom.

Some say a doubt is a doubt. It has no state of mind. A state of mind is attributed to it by 'us' - at times, even without knowing what the doubt is, without considering its relevance or otherwise to the objective. If only we make an effort on these lines before attributing a status to it, things would be much better. Maybe doubt is just our interpretation of, or label for, some external stimulus to switch on creativity?

The **RULES** to doubt: The Wise says, "If you doubt at first, doubt again." It means that any doubtful situation or thought should not be left unattended especially when the impact of that situation is possibly big. You cannot leave anything unaddressed which may put your activities/plans in jeopardy. Be skeptical in a constructive way to develop creativity continuously.

73

Assimilation

The ultimate aim of assimilating knowledge is to create new ideas or gain wisdom.

Generally speaking, assimilation is a cognitive process that manages how we take in new information or idea and integrate that into our existing knowledge. Knowledge assimilation and continuous adaptation are important to fuel creativity, and they help to widen the fields and the scope. It gives wings to the imagination and this, in turn, becomes things which help to connect the wild dots to spur creativity.

Knowledge should be helpful for imagination. Knowledge assimilation helps us understand how and what forces we are dealing with in our journey. Imagine what can be accomplished by increasing knowledge and applying it to what one has imagined.

Generally speaking, to identify a person's creativity potential, look for the strong evidence of a desire to learn and to grow. High potential people are intellectually curious, with the strong desire to learn, assimilate knowledge and expand their horizon, to discover unknown, or practice entrepreneurship.

From a business management perspective, innovation is production or adoption, assimilation, and exploitation of a value-added novelty in economic and social spheres; renewal and enlargement of products, services, and markets; development of new methods of production; and the establishment of new management systems.

The **RULEs** *for assimilation.* The ultimate aim of assimilating knowledge is to create new ideas or gain wisdom. The very theme for us is that our life is the journey with the knowledge we gain and the experience we assimilate, etc. Innovators assimilate all relevant and available information, transform them into insight, and consciously cultivate creativity as a habit.

74

Synthesis

Creativity is a synthesis of two qualities: imagination and concreteness.

Our mind is often dynamic and creative. The principle of creative synthesis was first mentioned by Wilhelm Wundt, a German physician, physiologist, philosopher, and professor, known today as one of the founding figures of modern psychology. A key feature of creative synthesis is that mental capacities are more than the sum of their parts, they are generative and creative. There is a real novelty in higher cognitive thought processes to spur creativity.

Creativity is a synthesis of two qualities: imagination with which you create new ideas and the concreteness with which you can transform ideas into real works. Synthesis is about understanding a thing by examining it as a whole. Creative solutions via synthesis are made from a much broader and encompassing view that is not possible in linear or analytical thinking only.

Digital is about hyperconnectivity and interdependence. Interconnections and interdependencies are distinguished, wise choices and decisions are made via the full cycle of analytics and synthesis. The essence of innovation is made of trying new combinations of known things. It's the essence of evolution.

Organizations need to allow time for a number of different 'creative' activities or opportunities to suit different types of people. In the same way, that people have different 'learning' styles, they also have different innovation styles. Each human being is a potential innovation by definition as you won't find two humans that are exactly the same. We are all new combinations of the known.

The **RULEs to make synthesis**: Creativity demands the possibility of the wrong in order to be exploring in a free and playful way. Creative people use specific systems to be creative with the emergent, divergent, convergent thought processes and so on. Diversity is always there to increase the probability of such synthesis.

75

Collaboration

Collaboration stimulates creativity and fuels sustainable growth.

Human's progress is made through three stages: dependent, independent, and interdependent; the higher state being is the collaborative interdependent one. Limited hierarchy works best in a creative environment where the free flow of ideas and their prompt implementation is a key element of success. It is about individual mental set-up too, hence, interdependent collaboration is a premium stage.

Today's situation calls for a new way of thinking and the next level of relationships and collaborations - between you and your work, you and your employer, you and yourself. Creative thinking is required and, quite possibly, a lot more nerve. To continuously innovate within individuals, groups, and organizations, you need to connect and communicate more openly, easily and effectively. From there, they need to work together efficiently on implementing ideas to deliver value. This collective action enhances the innovation experience and leads to higher diffusion rate.

Communities based on mutual interest encourage close collaboration. These communities can be engaged in offering ideas, enhancing these ideas by combining and building upon one another to shape solutions and work together to implement resulting innovations. Innovation communities, then, become a transformational catalyst to diffuse new kinds of thinking throughout an organization.

The **RULEs** _for collaboration_: Collaboration helps improve creativity, quality, reliability and also productivity; it helps stimulate creativity and fuel sustainable growth. Everyone has a valuable contribution to make at whatever level in the formal hierarchy they happen to be placed, the goal for optimized organizational design is to get the mass collaboration, innovation through less hierarchy, cross-functional insight and adopt a socialization process designed for the globally connect the world.

76

Solitude

Creativity flourishes in solitude.

Creativity is a thinking activity, solitude nurtures creativity. In quietness, you can hear your thoughts, you can reach deep within yourself, and you can focus. Further, the quietness of mind comes from self-discipline that ensures the train of thoughts has wider gaps to perceive such unique signals and also a strong capacity to catch and store these signals before they leave us.

We all coexist in one space. The quiet space is in alignment with nature and nature is in alignment with the quiet space; we are in a creative harmony with one another despite all of our differences. There is nature's calming quiet. The sound of the wind and birds sounding their own symphony, seeing the different gradients of green on the land and in the water and the different gradients of blue in the sky and the ocean. In this natural space, all that is present including self is different from each other.

Despite having no control over what naturally occurs, the peace of mind and heart exist in space. Space and silence although at first glance might be dismissed as "nothing," they are all around us-even if we can't see them. When under challenge, you need the peace and tranquility to keep creativity flow, seek assurances on decisions, and intentions. You can build internal abilities to find creativity, peace, and space...

The **RULEs** to create silence and spark creativity

: Creativity flourishes in solitude. In quietness, you can hear your thoughts, you can reach deep within yourself, and you can focus. There is "no one-size fits all" solution of creating space and silence in our lives, and more importantly to ask ourselves: What value do we place on creating quiet space and silence? Then put our answer to the question of - Is valuing and creating space and quiet silence in my daily routine in alignment with my health and peace of mind? With silence, the mind gets focused and the creativity can be switched on.

77

Reflection

Self-reflection is an important stage to diagnose, develop and strengthen your creativity.

Self-awareness has generally been viewed as an individual attribute, it's the introspect and ability to understand your own personality, emotion, thought processes, habit. etc. Knowing who you are and how you react and respond in different situations can help you understand and improve the cognitive, relational and assertive actions you take on a day to day basis, for either developing creativity or improving learning agility.

You are just these things; body, mind, emotion, and energy. Right now, the combination of these elements is what you call "self." The mind is the output as ideas, opinions, feelings, emotions, attitude are attributes of one's behaviors. The human thought process is controlled and limited by internal and external factors. Ask yourself questions that focus on knowing thyself and continuously practice on how to recharge your energy, boost your creativity, strengthen your strength, also not make your weakness become the obstacle to stop you from moving forward or leading effectiveness. This has helped you in understanding how you can do a change of self that will positively reflect anyone around you.

Self-reflection is crucial in scrutinizing on how you are doing to develop creativity and make decisions. The problem is with having the ability to reflect over how you make sense of something, to identify cognitive gaps, potential blind spots, to reflect your process of sense making as a way to query the relevance and boundaries of the prejudice you have used in your judgment process. It is possible to think about systems from both micro and macro perspective in a systematic fashion, to connect the reasonable dots, you cannot observe what you do not know. Recognition cannot function without cognition.

The RULEs for reflection: Through self-reflection, you can connect more valuable dots, see the trees without missing the forest; understand the big pictures without ignoring the significant details, to boost creativity and grow into full maturity.

78

Prioritization

Prioritization provides a framework for focusing on creativity.

Creativity can be in the form of an idea, a solution, and an approach. Prioritization is about managing constraints - you can't do everything; so which projects will you do? In general, prioritization increases creativity and does not decrease it. But the term has a different semantic connotation, and each situation is different, so there is always going to be lots of different opinions.

The prioritization mind can stay focus; spend time and energy on activities to cultivate creativity. It is an important thinking skill for today's multitasking, multi-devicing digital workforce because they are more empowered to apply their knowledge and be accountable to what they choose to work on, how to get it done, and understand the purpose of work, to cultivate creativity and build professional competency.

Creativity typically comes from having some resources that you can apply to problem-solving. From innovation management perspective, there're always some constraints for businesses to explore the new opportunities or deploy the new ideas, therefore, evaluation and prioritization are taken place to leverage resources in innovation management. It is up to the idea proposed to show it is worthwhile. The key is to separate 'Evaluation' of ideas from "Prioritization."

Prioritization brings transparency to the organization and creates internal competition among new ideas and projects. Prioritization forces people to be more creative, to come up with better ideas. Evaluation is where creativity lives or eliminated - depending on the nature, culture, and needs of the organization. In addition, prioritization helps to focus the strategy of the organization, which has huge benefits in terms of execution.

Prioritization is also the process and method that one communicates either top down or bottom up and impacts on how a creative approach, idea, or project is received in an organization. If you have two somewhat conflicting needs - high quality and low cost, for example, you can apply creative techniques to achieve both.

*The **RULEs** for setting prioritization to focus on innovation:* Prioritization provides a framework to focus on creativity. It encourages spending more time on creativity-related activities or laser focus on innovation-driven management via leveraging limited resource- "Doing more with innovation."

79

Commitment

Make time and space commitment for things matter, including how to unlock your creativity.

Creativity is a constructive disruption, as well as a fine addiction. Creativity has become #1 most needed professional skill in the 21st century. The more opportunity employees have to use their mind, to connect the dots, unlock creativity, and take responsibilities, the more fulfilled they will be. It is about shaping an idea that comes with a commitment to push it through, with personal dynamics and guts, determination and single-mindedness.

At the organizational level, the high-level of leadership commitment is important to orchestrate collective creativity via building a culture of innovation. Shared accountability involves shared ownership because most breakdowns stem from silo behavior where people aren't coordinating, communicating, solving problems in a way that considers consequences to others. Accountability needs to be a two-way commitment that does need to consider real empowerment levels to encourage creativity. True accountability focuses on learning to do things differently.

When business leaders, regardless what type of mind you have, goes beyond short-term gain, take a calculated risk and make a long-term commitment, organizations have a better opportunity to become highly innovative. Innovative organizations naturally have closer connections between functions and all functions and levels are more intimately involved with the market and each other on a regular basis. Policies, processes, and commitment (resources, not words) from top management should establish and foster curiosity with the cross-pollination of ideas and a close connection to the market for all parts of the organization.

<u>The **RULEs** to make a commitment</u>: Allow autonomy; let people choose how and on what they work, to unlock creativity. People want to feel part of something great, and they want to feel that they are making a significant contribution to that greatness. When they feel this way, they not only become energized by challenges, they can also endure much greater pressures and demands without becoming burnt out, make a commitment, and become more creative.

80

Perception

Perception shows how deep one can understand an issue or a phenomenon, the mental strength.

Creativity is the inward journey to shape a new idea. No one may dare to claim he or she has decoded creativity or can see through the creativity, but each one of us can perceive, understand, and experience innovation via our own unique lens. Perception is based on one's thought processes which are influenced by one's thinking style, cognitive understanding, and knowledge level.

Historian: Genuine innovation is only decided by history. It requires thinking beyond, as opposed to outside the box, altering or changing the frame of reference to create previously unconsidered solutions.

Entrepreneur: Innovation is the process of commercializing, not just coming up with ideas. The latter is actually in abundance - the entrepreneurial and intrapreneurial ability to deliver it.

Philosopher: Innovation is to see the substance of things unseen. One can see an egg another sees an omelet, to be innovative is to transform the single thread into a beautiful garment, words to poetry, ideas expanded to create more ideas, to create concepts.

Futurist: Innovator foresees the future and helps make it happen.

Mathematician: Innovations is to see in which circumstances one plus one is not equal to two.

Scientist: *Innovation is simply solving an old problem in a new way.*

Engineer: Innovation is to make complexity simple, think how to be and make the most complex things of this world simple, it's the creative destruction, not the other way around.

Cosmologist: Innovation is not always a rocket science.

Firefighter: Innovation is the flame we can keep it firing up.

Chef: Innovation is about to make a tasteful and unique dish with the regular ingredients.

Parent: Innovation is the love child of insight and imagination.

Lazy Boy or Girl: innovation is the result of laziness (or laziness is the mother of innovation).

Chapter 5 Motivational Ingredients

Innovation is about moving forward. If you are not moving forward, you are moving backward. There is no standing still.

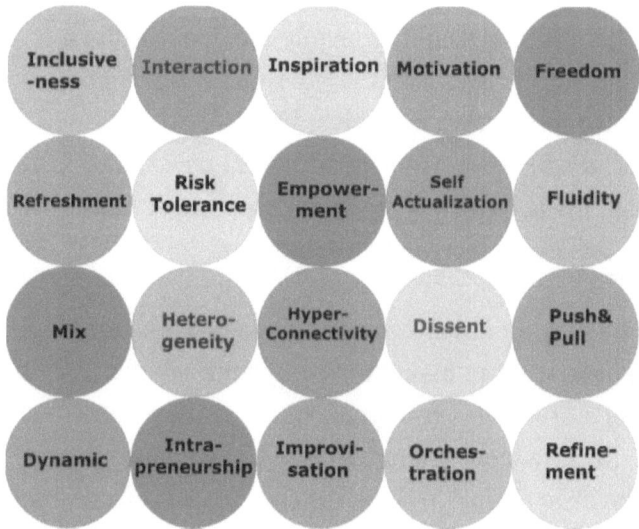

Figure 6 Motivational Ingredients

Creativity has many forms and manifestations. Take the standpoint that creativity has its starting point within an individual. Creativity can manifest in a collective environment. While the individual contributions provide the 'building block' of creativity, it is the collective consensus on what to do with them that is exciting. Once we take into consideration the influences around this person (environment, culture, education, etc.), their creativity will manifest in different forms.

Creativity is a function of imagination, knowledge, psychology, activities, and evaluation. However, besides those ingredients, the most important element is the attitude put to increase the chance of generating creative ideas. One of the aspects of creativity is the environment where individuals or groups need to generate creative results regularly and frequently, with the pressure of time. The motivation for innovation is not just because it would make work better. It's because of the need, the urgency, the competition, the acquisition of some new capacity that creates the difference between "should" and "is."

Everyone displays innovation at some stage, some more often than others; some make more impact than others. It is the manager's or leader's role to encourage and nurture those who display these characteristics - individuals that have the intrinsic ability to think outside the box. And it is important to update talent management practices and performance measurement to encourage creativity and inspire learning, exploring and innovating.

From creativity starting within an individual to the point where it becomes external to them (visually, aurally, tactilely, etc.), it cannot be identical from one person to another. And by manifesting creativity from an individual endeavor to a team activity and a collective effort, the horizon of creativity is expanded, it converges with the concept of innovation that is the management discipline to transform innate ideas and achieve its business value

81

Inclusiveness

Being inclusive means to appreciate differences and enjoy the diverse viewpoints.

Creativity is about being different. If you start from a point of, "We are all different - with different gifts and skills," and then the opportunities open up, not close down. Inclusiveness is the must to build a culture of creativity. Many organizations themselves are restricting the diversity by simply selecting those people that reflect their current culture and norms. Where the focus needs to be is in how they incorporate true diversity into the businesses in order to spark creativity, to foster a culture of open-mindedness, to the best of ability.

Secondly, look at the creativity at a group level and assume similar levels of competencies and capabilities, would a diverse group of people come up with a more out-of-the-box idea/solution than a group of identical people? By generating scenarios where there is no one solution to one problem, but rather to construct an event where the individual inputs must compound and build upon each other, you can observe a creative result that was beyond the capacity of any one individual.

Thirdly, try to include a diverse team of participants in your ideation processes as possible. Look out for curious people with a broad knowledge base, a hands-on attitude and good analytic and social skills. Make your creative processes available to everybody. Ask people what initiatives they will take to handle diversity in the workplace. Fill the driving seat, and have designated staff to run, manage and curate your ideation processes. Also, deal with stereotypes by showing people that even two people within the same family can be different. Hence, it is wrong to stereotype against a whole population of a particular group.

Acceptance is not the purpose or goal of inclusiveness. Rather, valuing inclusiversity means acknowledging that other people, other races, other voices, and other cultures have as much integrity and as much claim in the world as you do. It is the recognition that there are other ways of seeing the world, solving problems, and working together.

The RULEs to be inclusive: You don't structure innovation. You apply principles of approach and vary the resource and tool mix by the ever-changing environment, day to day through the year to year. Creativity can be enhanced by a team with members who have diverse experiences. It is important to have members of the team with diverse experiences and who have worked with different systems and platforms and for both small and large corporations. In this case, where we are focusing on designing and implementing a specific application to be used by a wide range of user diversity is a major advantage.

82

Interaction

Creativity can manifest in a collective environment.

A creative person is one that offers the others a different perspective to look at the world, and creativity is realized in the process of interaction with others and the world. As the ability to work and produce, creativity then requires a certain degree of independence and mental balance, the proper psychological level of inner security and genuine autonomy.

Organizations and their people learn and are creative through their interactions with the environment. Creativity can manifest in a collective environment. While the individual contributions provide the 'building block" of creativity, it is the collective consensus on what to do with them that is exciting. They act, observe the consequences of their action, make inferences about those consequences, and draw implications for future action. The process is adaptively rational with the intention to manage innovation in a structural way.

Digitalization stipulates companies work together in a hyper-connected and continuously converging environment that provides structural processes and a certain extent of serendipity. The evolution of innovation only exists in these more open environments that harness interactions, create insights, take advantage of all sources of creativity in a more open way and make a leap of innovation management to the next level.

The **RULEs** to spark collective creativity:

Organizations are complex adaptive living systems, which are comprised, in part, of people (subsystems) who are also complex adaptive living systems, all such systems function, grow and prosper by continually learning, innovating, adapting, and evolving.

83

Inspiration

Inspiration is not just a short-term momentum. It could take time and generations of change to truly build a culture of creativity.

Each and every one of us is equipped with the huge capacity to be creative. Creative people are inspired to think and work nearly every day on creating and brainstorming, they are not waiting for the magical "Aha" moment, but proactively stimulate the new energy of fresh thinking and work diligently to develop their creativity.

Inspiration is to reflect who you are, compete for uniqueness. It takes the vision to pull up. At the individual level, the whole creative process can be frustrating because it's so nonlinear. Inspiration is a notch up from motivation because it's the urge to do something significantly different and with heart! Do you feel an inner urge to be creative? Do you like solving problems in novel ways? Perhaps you like investigating possibilities. Were you born wired for creativity or are you learning creativity as part of a quest to become a well-rounded person?

At the business level, highly innovative leaders inspire creativity and encourage thinking differently. From innovation management perspective, one of the difficulties here is the use of the words "creative" and "innovative." They are drastically different. Creativity is the innate process to create new ideas. Leaders can inspire and influence people to become more creative, but innovation management is also important because innovation is more about how to transform creative ideas and achieve its business value, often in the systematic way. Regarding the employee feelings and approval of the changing development if necessary, you need to challenge the status quo de facto standards, to inspire and reward creativity.

The RULEs to build an inspirational environment: While you can train somebody to become more innovative or, at least, understand the innovative thinking. It takes time and generations of changes within a company to embrace the fresh thinking and the new way to do things. Otherwise, there will always be roadblocks to these "new" ideas. Engage employees in strategy understanding, and inspire creativity.

84

Motivation

"To motivate" is the act of giving somebody a reason or incentive to do something.

Self-motivation is a significant component in the expression of creativity. While we each have the enormous creative capacity, our willingness to exercise and express it becomes more complicated. Motivating requires giving someone a 'motive,' usually self-interest along the line. Motivation is the "cognitive momentum" that comes from consistently applying the habits congruent with the achievement of the goal. Motivation can come and go just as easy if it is not the heart desire, a true passion, or an authentic expression.

Motivation is perhaps a combination of several emotions. Desire is the spearhead to motivation, which in turn creates the mind to wonder how to make your mission of change possible. It is the recognition that something is missing or something needs to be enhanced to get to the satisfaction level that you need or want. A desire mind is a necessary element of motivation to transform inward driven creativity into outward driven innovation.

Maybe you have to make certain what it is you are going after in that motivation. Having attributes of a leader in oneself will be the acumen. So is it easy to tell if the person is motivated or is full of fear? When a person is motivated by fear, the motivation is short lived. The only one who can motivate you is you. You have to have the desire and be willing to challenge yourself to be all you can be to unlock creativity.

In an organizational context, it's important to develop the process of a corporate pulse that identifies where the pulse/passion/motivation/commitment of the organization lies, and who embodies it - who is willing? Who is motivated out of fear? The purpose is the greatest motivator; a deep desire to make the world a better place and fueled by a sense of gratitude and responsibility that compels you to stay committed. When motivation seems to fade away sometimes, forgiveness of self first heals and recharges so does a good sense of humor.

The RULEs to build a motivational environment: Let people explore where their energy is and then align the energy to work at hand. Success, however, requires motivation, determination, persistence, dedication and practice in the present - right now.

85

Freedom

A free person is indeed "rule-less," "border-less," and "worry-less," but not thinking less or mindless.

When you don't have any compulsion, you are free. Before you can do that, you have to know who and what you are at this moment to even determine what the free expression of your constructed self is right now. You are free. You just seek. You try to find answers from within. You don't worry whether it's positive or negative, you accept things, you don't judge, you don't worry about what others think, you don't get into a rat race. You don't believe in any dogmas. Your mind is not cluttered. A free person is indeed "rule-less," "border-less," and "worry-less," but not thinking less or mindless, he or she can be more creative.

The creative mind is often free of psychological inertia. The mind needs to be freed so that it's connected to the rest of the universe and allows ideas to flow through. Every problem that we face has a similar or analogous problem in past, in some other industry, geography, or in a leading area. One just needs to find that existing solution and adapt it to the current problem.

However, most of the organizations today are process and control driven. Emphasis is on compliance with the result people forget to think freely. Why are organizations not realizing that the very process and controls instituted are emanated from the thought process of people; and to be robust and helpful, you must allow people to think and contribute to the design and restructure of the process.

In the end, however, freedom is freedom from compulsion or necessity, but for this to exist, we need morality and for morality to exist, we need an objective understanding of progress. "*She is free in her wildness, she is a wanderess, a drop of free water. She knows nothing of borders and cares nothing for rules or customs. 'Time' for her isn't something to fight against. Her life flows clean, with passion, like fresh water.*" -Roman Payne

The RULEs to create a working environment with freedom: The culture of the organization must nurture free thinking. The point is one cannot develop a right way within an environment that rewards wrong ways. Freedom ignites creativity, and creativity catalyzes human progress.

86

Refreshment

Creating space and silence, even for a moment, allows one to observe rather than act.

Creativity is the flow of energy. It is important to recharge our mind and restore our mental strength. Space and silence are keys to listening from the heart and refreshing the mind. It's the place where the dots often get connected and the transformation occurs.

Not only is our culture constantly changing, we are bombarded with and have learned to constantly seek information on the minutiae of every facet of each change. The problem is never to get new, innovative thoughts into your mind, but how to get old ones out. The critical information which we so often miss, though, is in the gaps. When we pause to take a breath, we have an opportunity to consolidate, assimilate and understand, but we usually view it simply as down or non-productive time. Without either creating or being consciously aware of the space and silence of the gaps, you are only able to achieve and facilitate incremental change.

The gap is where Eureka exists. With the space to breathe in moving through a big change, one is transforming the whole of you somehow, so is in danger of taking your breath away. People need some time to just fiddle around with ideas or new technologies. From our own personal experience that some of best ideas occur when we are "playing" the problem, of course, you need to show results as well.

To boost creativity energy, clearly you need a space to breathe again in the pathway for real change; it's critical for people to have time to breathe a new air that enables new sight and helps people see a different and new way of doing something.

The **RULEs** to create space and refresh the mind: Experience with mindful walking, create silence-listening from the heart, feel recharged and get inspired in quiet spaces and enjoy the peace of mind with silent moments.

87

Risk-Tolerance

Innovation by its inherent nature comes with a risk.

People tend to be "risk averse." With creativity, "change" is made." With every "change," the risk is involved. The more dramatic and powerful the change is, the greater the risk would be. The most important characteristic of being creative is to act without fear and let you self-conscious express itself.

Without the acceptance of failure, creativity and innovation will suffer. And if we want creativity, we must build in the acceptance, even the celebration of small, quick failures. Innovation by its inherent nature comes with a risk. The failure is of crucial importance in the process of achieving innovation, as so many of the greatest thinkers in the history have identified, people learn far deeper and more enduring lessons from significant failures than from anything else. The best judgment, a qualitative approach is given for risk and innovation.

From innovation management perspective, create a fearless and diversified working environment to spur creativity. Employees need to be given 'permission' to be innovative.

Failure should be regarded as a learning experience rather than offense. However, in many organizations, creativity, curiosity, trust and strong relationship with consumers, that should be leading any company's decision, come to the bottom of priorities ladder.

The RULEs to build a risk-tolerance culture:

Certainly innovation that brings out new products or spots a niche should be rewarded. Failure should not be an offense and actually, if there are not a few failures, then you are not trying hard enough. The job of management is to help when a failure happens to turn it around as a team. Build the culture of continuous learning and encourage breakthrough thinking.

88

Empowerment

Create a working atmosphere to allow free expressing the creative potentials.

Creativity needs to be encouraged and creative peoples need to be empowered. To stay healthy in an environment of the workplace, there need emotional guarantees that only a peaceful climate and a good communication can provide. The emotional well-being in the workplace allows everyone to express the best of themselves, makes one feel good and makes one more creative to get jobs well done.

Manage to create an innovative atmosphere, starting from the top is necessary, so everyone can express themselves freely and unlock their creative potential, have the career satisfaction and improve the results in terms of production. C-levels have a clear vision and want to maximize creativity and innovation at all levels in the organization to grow their organization, realizing not all might wish to do so. It also depends on the innovation skills of managers and also of all employees.

The biggest reason most organizations are not more creative is that the vast majority of senior managers simply don't know how to get there. It requires shared vision plus innovative, committed and passionate leadership and a commitment to alignment and integration of people, processes, practices and technologies across the enterprise, including customer and vendor engagement.

*The **RULEs** to build a working environment with empowerment:* There is no one size fits all recipe to engage in the existing practices, introduce and reinforce the changes to build a culture of creativity. Each person wants and needs to know, understands and be willing to be a part of the transformation. Hiring winners is an essential part of growth and being successful, but the real challenge is transforming the existing workgroups, departments, and facilities into creative and high performers.

89

Self-actualization

Self-realization is a desire to experience ever deeper fulfillment by realizing and actualizing more of own potential.

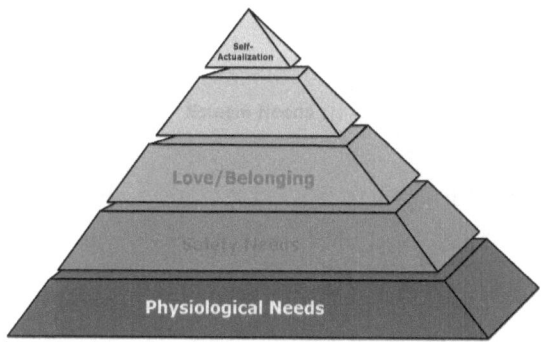

Figure 7 The Maslow's Hierarchy

Maslow's Hierarchy of Needs Model summarized five tiers and self-actualization was at the top of the triangle (Physiological Needs-Safety Needs-Social Needs-Esteem Needs-Self Actualization Needs), and later the 6th tier was added to the top of the model: Self-transcendence; which is to experience, and unify with and serve that is beyond the individual self.

Digital is the age of mastery, digital technologies amplify the talent's voice and leadership influence, track the internet citizens' digital footprint and knowledge fluency, innovation now is everyone's game and collective wisdom is the power of the crowd.

The author of "*Drive,*" Daniel Pink suggests that a few simple, motivational factors govern the reasons we work and the reasons we work "willingly and well." He divides these motivational factors into three core elements:
- Autonomy: People need autonomy over the task, time, team and technique elements of their work.
- Mastery: This can be boiled down to engagement and mastery or "flow." More specifically, the need to constantly build upon and improve one's skills and use them in a work setting.
- Purpose: The humans love to feel what we do is for the purpose of something that is greater than ourselves, the inner force to harmonize and unify.

The RULEs to build a working environment for encouraging self-actualization: Leaders need to well align employees' professional goals with the strategic goals of the business. Employees are already paid to put their time, effort and skills for the company to make the contribution to the organization's success, and at the same time, to climb the Maslow's pyramid, for discovering purposes, achieving self-actualization, cultivating capabilities and mastering skills.

90

Fluidity

Creativity is fluid, like fountainhead from within you, flowing out.

Digital means flow, data flow, information flow, knowledge flow, mind flow, and business flow. Organizations, like individuals, need to be in flow to operate smoothly. Digital boundaries are not "sharp" lines; they are fluid to adapt to changes.

From an organizational structure perspective, an organization achieves this state of equilibrium through its management layers. The rigid organizational structure stifles innovation and in many large legacy organizations, there are layers upon layers of bureaucracy ensuring that creativity will go nowhere. No matter how much the enacting company pays lip service to their ability to support and build toward innovation. In the end, the entire structure of the large business is designed to reject creativity flow because they don't contribute quantifiably to the execution of their current business model.

Delayering becomes a lens through which it is possible to examine and then fix many other issues including innovation stagnation. In other words, an organization can approach the flow zone when the positions in its hierarchy have clear, accountable tasks. The latest enterprise social platforms and collaboration tools make it practical to break down functional silos and improve cross-functional communication and collaboration.

The RULEs to build a "fluid" environment.

The creativity and mastery of innovation are more as flow than dominance. The true mastery doesn't mean dominance over, but where we flow with, and yet manipulate to our desire and higher best interest. It is important to cultivate the learning culture that has awareness and understanding plus setting a new behavior expectation of proactive participants. The emergent digital technologies such as social platform provide a flexible way to learn, share and collaborate, with the very goals to groom future leaders, innovators, and foster employee engagement and development.

91

Mix

Digital has the hybrid nature; it's about mixing something old and new, the best practices and the next practices.

Creativity has a language, but it is altogether different from the one found in the business environment. There is an idea of "productive friction" and "creative tension" via building an innovative team with mixing cognitive differences, personalities, skills, or capabilities, as a way of encouraging and instilling a creative environment.

The digital balance of human nature will need to have some combination of structural design and incentives. The "organizational design problem" would be to build the "best" mix of organizational elements that enable a living digital organization for keeping creativity flow and improving innovation success rate. The digital strategy represents the demand side of organizational design as it points toward the cross-border synergies that need to be developed to spark creativity. These synergies require effective and efficient cross-border organizational interdependence.

The challenge for organizations is to manage its portfolio of relevant cross-border strategic synergies and organizational interdependence with the appropriate mix of enabling organizational elements - people, process, and technology, engaging digital talent in innovation and balancing creativity and efficiency, innovation and standardization.

The RULEs to make a highly creative mixed team: Creating a great mix and maintaining the digital balance is a never-ending business life-cycle. From talent management perspective, promoting people based on taking advantage of the opportunities for horizontal and lateral engagements is likely to be a core principle for actually building creative digital organizations.

92

Heterogeneity

The exercise of blending people's cognitive differences and problem-solving abilities to produce the desired outcome is a worthwhile thing to do.

Heterogeneity is the digital characteristic of today's organizations. A highly diverse group almost always accelerates innovation dramatically as well as spurs general creativity. The exercise of blending people's cognitive differences and problem-solving abilities to produce the desired outcome is a worthwhile thing to do.

Managers are taught to manage process and resources effectively to manage innovation in a structural way. Variance by personality, function, industry experience, role, and audience allow for superior need discovery, ranking and business model creation, assessment, and validation. It is not just a mere accumulation of the creative inputs of those involved. It is also not only about synchronizing their individual inputs to make something that no one individual would achieve. It is more than that. It has its own dynamic that is in a state of constant flux. It builds up a momentum that draws creative contributions from the participants that they did not previously conceive or understood they were capable of.

Whether creativity can be collective is clear and flows from what seems like an expansive, generous, creative mind, and illustrates the 'Third Alternative' synergistic result Steven Covey, the author of *"7 Habits of Highly Effective People"* refers to when the final result is bigger than the intentions of the individuals involved. It is indeed creative to push, invite, allow, and accept ideas from a group to reach a final result not originally predicted because it requires the openness to create a new idea and allow it to form fully.

The RULEs to embrace heterogeneity:

Organizations should empower all sorts of innovative talents. You need out-of-the-box thinkers, creative problem solvers, change agents, customer champions and digital orchestrators; and those who can connect unusual dots, think forward, dig deeper, see through the issues, look around and beneath the corner, and work smarter.

93

Hyperconnectivity

Digital is the age of innovation because creativity is about connecting the dots in the wider scope.

Creativity is about connecting the dots. In life, we come across various experiences, exposure to various situations, as wider dots. The more dots you have, the better chance your mind can connect them freely. The digital workforce today is hyper-connected and divergent in many ways; share a natural affinity for new perspectives, innovations, and collective wisdom.

Digital is about connectivity, it means to have the better ability for dots connection across the knowledge domains, geographical, functional, organizational, industrial, or generational boundaries. Digital is the age of innovation because creativity is about connecting the dots in the wider scope. How cleverly you connect your dots by leveraging your experiences and finding a solution to the problems is creativity which is also an important aspect of digital fluency.

Hyperconnectivity keeps creativity flow and drives innovation frictionlessly. If one of your employees came up with a new initiative to start an ideation process on a certain question, where would he or she take it? How to keep the ideas flow, and therefore, innovation flow? You need to know how to involve employees, and how to manage ideas and implement them seamlessly.

The RULEs to harness hyper-connectivity:

Hyper-connectivity brings both the abundance of opportunities and unprecedented risks. Hence, connecting means to discern the trend from fads, keep creativity flow, seek business values before taking business initiatives, to build a hyper-connected and high-innovative digital powerhouse.

94

Dissent

There is always a right way to challenge others and it is never demeaning, always constructive.

People consciously or subconsciously protect their status quo. To be truly creative means challenging conventional wisdom and beliefs. Creativity needs dissent and conflict. It is likely that if you are creative, you will challenge the status quo as you push the parameters of the norms of life.

We are living in a complex world where inventions, developments, and conflicts are continuously changing and that makes it impossible to have complete knowledge and understanding of any issue. We all bring different perspectives and our boundaries might have changed based on the open conversations and taking the time to thoughtfully think about the specific issue of boundaries.

Constructive dissent catalyzes creativity and therefore human progress. Having conflicts in the team is sometimes productive as well if it could lead to open-minded discussion for alternative problem-solving and it creates a sense of positive competition in the team, and a number of times, a lot of new ideas come up from these constructive conflicts. The team's creativity is amplified via talented people with the cognitive difference; they can understand things from different angles and bring new perspectives to the table. It is also not only about synchronizing of their individual inputs to make something that no one individual would achieve. It is even more than that; it has its own dynamic that is in a state of constant flux.

Since innovation is fundamentally about breaking assumptions, having more assumptions uncovered will lead to greater innovation. As we bring more people into the dialog, we increase the probability of those various assumptions surfacing as each person filters different things. Of course, that only works if those people are somewhat different from one another. Collaborating with entirely like-minded people probably won't yield results. The more diversified the team is, the more innovative the collaboration can turn to be.

The **RULEs** to encourage constructive dissent and spark creativity: Encourage people to question the status quo, think independently and create an environment that encourages dissent and candor. There is always a right way to challenge others and it is never demeaning, always constructive. Life without challenges is boring and may lead to change inertia, negative attitudes, and poor behaviors accordingly.

95

Push and Pull

To succeed in driving innovation, it is essential for empowering people to push ideas forward, and the entire company to be pulling in the right direction.

Good ideas are multidimensional, so execution also needs forces of both push and pull. Ideas take root in unsuspected places and they evolve with time and by unexpected connections. People need permission to push ideas around an organization without the fear of failure and without the need to deliver against a short-term narrow - focused objective. It is also critical to pulling the resources to build an innovation nurturing working environment.

The rigorous innovation structures are supported by the right policies and programs. Keep hierarchy as low as possible. Cut the politics. There are times fostering a culture where creativity thrives really helps drive innovation that can fit into an existing business or process.

However, the reality is that the organizational structures and relationships with and between employees were designed for a very different age. Most organizations are grossly dysfunctional, despite often noble attempts at change or innovation by the leadership team. More often, workers are asked to be "engaged" inside and outside the company environment, at the same time, many companies don't have the mechanisms or interest in engaging employees in enabling personal growth, and implementing a platform or methodology that unleashes their creativity potentials.

The **RULEs** to manage innovation via "Push and Pull":

The bottom line is, for any company to succeed in innovation, it is essential for the entire company to be pulling in the right direction, and people need to be empowered to push ideas forward. Innovation dilemmas can only be solved by strong innovation leaders who understand these challenges and work to build a digital-ready organizational culture and structure to eliminate barriers and mind gaps to open the new chapter of innovation blossom.

96

Dynamic

Digital workplace is dynamic, fluid, live, creative, flexible, and productive.

Due to the "VUCA" characteristics of digital new normal, digital workplace today needs to become dynamic and innovative. Complacency is probably the biggest challenge either individuals or organizations have to overcome. Because organizations and individuals that are complacent do not look for new opportunities or hazards. Winning in the digital dynamic means engaging innovative thinking, and building the strong collaboration. People have to be ready for moving to a more fluid state via overcoming change inertia and stepping out of "Comfort Zones."

All elements of risk-taking propensity and also proactive behavior will lead towards innovation. You have to remember that innovation can be a breakthrough and notice that it requires a "break." They include being a risk taker, challenging the status quo, being fearless, keeping dynamic, and looking at failure as a learning opportunity, and always looking for a better way to do things.

Digital workplace is dynamic, fluid, live, creative, flexible, and productive. Organizations need to invest in the cultivation of capacity for innovation. A leader encourages innovation, gives the freedom to employees to do anything new and even if it fails, they learn from it and grow only to do better in the future, and that is where innovation thrived in every little thing they did.

The RULEs to build a dynamic workplace:

The workplace needs to be designed to help employees at all levels within an organization (from top leaders to front-line employees) understand and develop their creative capacity to solve problems and explore opportunities in new and innovative ways. No one innovates alone. You need synergy and collaborative teams with "liquid" talent flowing to where it's needed.

97

Intrapreneurship

Intrapreneurialism is a constructive emotion that drives positive value creation in the well-established organizations.

Intrapreneurship is about practicing entrepreneurship in well-established organizations. Compared to nimble startups, many well-established organizations are struggling with innovation, due to the legacy technologies or processes, silo thinking, change inertia, or rigid hierarchy.

Intrapreneurship is about creating the future via learning, experimenting, and discovering. Innovation follows basic rules, which are adapted depending on the company's situation and ambition. People can learn tools to develop both their divergent and convergent thinking skills. They can learn to generate more novel and useful ideas in diverse teams. Intrapreneurialism is a constructive emotion that drives positive value creation in the organization and breaks mindsets that prevent risk happening and so potentially stifle real innovation.

In the 20th century, entrepreneurs and professional managers act more like different breeds of leaders; entrepreneurs think out of the box, professional managers set up and manage within the box; entrepreneurs break the rules, professional managers make the policies and play the politics, entrepreneurs dream big to make the dent in the universe, and professional managers keep focusing on winning finance results; entrepreneurs present resilience; professional managers manage elasticity; actually, in order to embrace and adapt to today's digital dynamic with paradoxical nature, such two sets of leadership characteristics are not exclusive, but complement each other.

Intrapreneur leaders often have balanced viewpoints to perceive success and failure objectively, such mental toughness will help an organization to be more resilient, and nurture the culture of risk-tolerance. Management should direct workflow, support the health of the team, create an environment where people want to work, encourage brainstorming. If management is successful, innovation will follow.

The RULEs to build intrapreneurship.

Develop employees entrepreneurially. Let them do things and solve problems in their own way to meet good results. Though the guide is needed at that crucial time; find the new stars and let them drive. Business innovation is bravery - it may take you to a whole other place, and you will see the innovation blossom in your organization.

98

Improvisation

Essentially, innovation is a type of creative disruption.

In the world of continual change, no one has all the answers. In fact, solutions often come from the floor and not the ceiling. Therefore, organizations need to support the process of improvisation which means "Accept what is given," "and "Build on what you have."

Innovation is the result of some kind of disruption; innovation can be defined as the collision between different perspectives, internal programming, mind-states of possibility and necessity and thought patterns that result in creative ideas and solutions.

You can feel creative tension when you sense the freedom to be creative, the harmony not via compliance only, but through idea sharing. People make creative communication often via asking open questions to explore new possibilities. To spark creativity, your digital workforce with heterogeneous team setting includes all sorts of thinkers: creative thinker, critical thinker, systems thinker, holistic thinker, paradoxical thinker, etc. They would complement each other's thought processes to stimulate collective creativity and amplify the collective human capabilities.

The **RULEs** to build an improvisational environment. Part of creating an organizational

environment that facilitates creativity involves paying attention to employee well-being and building individual emotional intelligence to generate more positive emotions and reducing unnecessary organizational pressures, have the right dose of creative tension and healthy competition to spark innovation.

99

Orchestration

Creative collaboration via integrative diversity and seamless orchestration can overcome silos.

Creativity is about thinking differently and doing things differently. And it ought to be remembered that there is nothing more difficult to take in hand, more perilous to conduct, or more uncertain in its success than to take the lead in the introduction of a new order of things. Because the innovator has enemies, those who have done well under the old conditions, those who do not readily believe in new things until they have had a long experience of them.

One of the biggest challenges in this complex digital world is the fact that we need different perspectives, different knowledge and different ways to solve a problem. Innovation is the teamwork, which can be orchestrated via interdisciplinary understanding, integrative diversity, and cross-functional collaboration. Silos stifle innovation. Silos are inevitable in every structured organization; silos are a method of containment and storage; bounded groups or insular tribes are evidence of silos, and silos are reservoirs for homogeneous thinking, limiting the organization's creativity and innovation.

It is the responsibility of the leaders to initiate their team to inspire creativity, break down the silos and orchestrate an innovation symphony. Companies must compete by creating corporate cultures and 'labs' with fertile ground for new ideas to sprout. The point is that corporations need to adapt and evolve by focusing on their core competency, which given all factors that are commoditized, boils down to creativity.

The **RULEs** *to orchestrate digital innovation symphony*: The highly complex and dynamic system needs to be orchestrated in a well-organized effort, brings organizations into the full-spectrum of dynamic capabilities, maturity challenges, paradoxes, pathologies across individuals, teams, looser groups, organizations, network-enterprises, and holistic digital ecosystems.

100

Refinement

Creativity is a good mix of art and science.

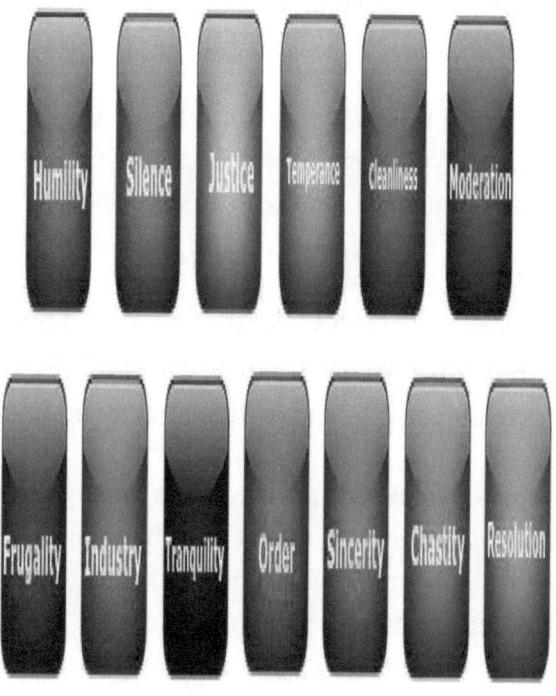

Figure 8 Refinement

According to Benjamin Franklin's thirteen virtues for insight in the creative process: If you consider the creative process, a process of refinement then all challenges, failures or successes are possible outcomes.

A positive attitude in the creative process to redefine, reinvent, re-innovate one's commitment to creativity is key. Perhaps challenges or failures can be considered part of the learning curve. In the art and design practice, the creative problem solving is a process in critical thinking. If you are committed to excellence, then all outcomes are the inspiration for future new developments.

Innovation, the very process to transform novel ideas and achieve the business value, in general, is surely a discipline. It covers innovation management, knowledge, and technology transfer, entrepreneurship and it is closely related to several other disciplines. It stands in between management, economy, psychology, sociology, and law, not speaking about disciplines that are related to technologies implemented by the particular innovation.

It's more a matter of focus and refinement to what you want to accomplish. Having lots of ideas is not a bad thing. The problems start when people start to choose the best idea of them to implement. If you remember that ideas are built on other ideas and that idea combination is a powerful technique, then having a big amount of ideas is a good thing as long as you then try and get the best attributes of the ones you like and combine them into one solid implementation and outcome.

The **RULEs** _for refinement:_ It would be helpful to study Benjamin's Franklin's thirteen virtues for insight in attitude toward success in the creative process: Humility, Silence, Justice, Temperance, Cleanliness, Moderation, Frugality, Industry, Tranquility, Order, Sincerity, Chastity, and Resolution.

Conclusion

Unlock Creativity via Daily Practices

Set your own principles, practice, practice, and practice more to ignite the abundance of creativity.

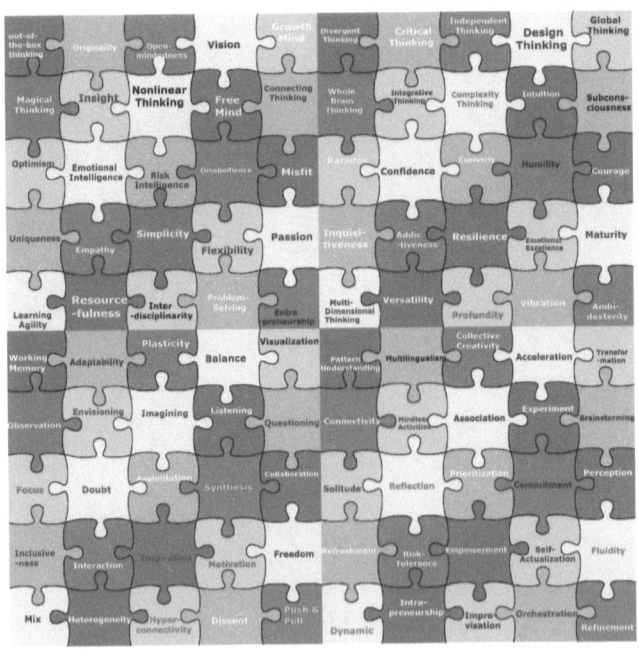

Figure 9 100 Creativity Ingredients

The life journey is like the childhood games we played, to draw the circle, paint the colors, or connect the dots, and unlock our innate creativity. Creativity becomes significantly important in the age with the advanced technologies because the digital workforce of the future will not be mere automatons, but continue to discover, explore, and improve the surroundings. The creativity suspends or defers judgment. However, it doesn't mean creativity lack of the principles, the well-set disciplines can streamline the train of the diversified thoughts and the continuous practices can unlock the fountain of creativity.

- **Blend unique ingredients to fuel creativity**: As we discussed in this book, there are many unique ingredients to make "creativity formula." There is a combination of intrinsic and extrinsic elements to ignite creativity. Creative people leverage emergent, divergent, and convergent thought processes to trigger creativity. On one hand, you need to have the level of curiosity, desire to learn, observe, with the natural ability to maintain an open and inquisitive mind; and on the other hand, it is important to have a motivational environment to encourage creativity, with less restricted rules, innovative leadership, and learning culture to empower innovators, bridge cognitive gaps, fertilize growth mindset and let creative minds soar.

- **Cultivate a thinking habit:** Creativity is a high level of thinking, either consciously or subconsciously. Creativity is a flow, an abstract and an imagination. Creativity comes into play when we call upon our conscious mind with the intention to bring forth solutions from our unconscious mind. You can put creativity in a box and say it's "all just creativity," or you can pull it out of the box and look at it through different lenses. It's your perception. Set your own principles and practice, practice, and practice more to spur the abundance of creativity. Creativity is a symbol of life, people who thrive as creative problem-solvers have developed a series of habits to connect the dots effortlessly and trigger creativity frequently.

- **Creative problem-solving:** Creativity needs a problem; creative people are both problem finders and problem solvers. Creatives always challenge conventional wisdom by asking questions which often lead to discovering situations others do not see at first. The essential to questioning stimulates the creative sides of our brains in order to find answers. And creatives would also say that it involves allowing being part of a process of trial and error. Creativity demands the possibility of the wrong in order to be exploring in a free and playful way.

- **Get out of the "fear":** The ideas come and go and, above all, we must instead leave them free, do not be afraid to say what we think or make a fool, do not let that stop, be fooled if we must, because often we say something brilliant, and to do that serve only method and experience, and get out of the "fear" that blocks our own genius, learn how to liberate imagination and come up with a new approach to the world. The evolution of innovation only exists in the more open environments that create insights, take advantage of all sources of creativity in a more open way. Individuals need to step outside the box and challenge perception, push themselves to the limit, their limit.

- **Encourage creatives to rise to the top**: Unlocking creativity, in some ways, is a little closer to the inverse of gold panning, where the valuable ingredients fall to the bottom, in that you are attempting to encourage the creatives to rise to the top and identify themselves. The complexity of this analogy kicks in when you consider that most well-meaning people are able to transform themselves from mud to gold through their conscious behavior. It is only when all individuals challenge themselves and then come together as a group will we see real human potential achieved.

If in the past the creativity was considered as a rare phenomenon and mysterious, it is now thought that, although with different gradation, is the heritage of all individuals. So, every person has the ability to be creative, just tearing down the mental barriers they have and tapping in their inherent abilities. Creativity is the potential which can be unlocked and innovation is the serendipity which can be unpuzzled. It comprises a combination of "flavored ingredients" that work together, flow, fluctuate, in harmony, in order to weave such creativity.

Acknowledgement

Writing a book is a journey taking 1% of inspiration and 99% of perspiration. *"100 Creativity Ingredients"* was born in the digital era, with the purpose to analyze special creativity ingredients, brainstorm the magical "creativity formula," and unpuzzle creativity in a structural way.

The purpose of "**100 Creativity Ingredients - Everyone's Playbook to Unlock Creativity** " is to classify, scrutinize, articulate, and share insight about one hundred special creativity ingredients, to paint the picture with them, to add colors on them, to embed the music into them, and to make the story via them, in order to unlock our collective creativity potential.

The content of *100 Creativity Ingredients* is based on years of research, numerous professional debates and brainstorming regarding innovation, leadership, talent management, and digitization, etc. I am deeply thankful to all for generously giving thoughts and wisdom.

Also, thanks for the courtesy images from **Pixabay.**

About the Author

Pearl Zhu is an innovative "Corporate Global Executive" with more than twenty-one years of technical and business working experience in strategic planning, Information Technology, software development, e-commerce and international trading, etc. Pearl Zhu is the author of "Digital Master" book series (12+Books), which include:
Digital Master –Debunk the Myth of Enterprise Digital Maturity,
CIO Master – Unleash the Digital Potential of IT,
Digital Valley – Five Pearls of Wisdom to Make Profound Influence,
Digital Agility-The Rocky Road from Doing Agile to Being Agile,
Leadership Master - Five Digital Themes to Leap Leadership Maturity,
Talent Master - 199+ Questions to See Talent from Different Angles,
Digitizing Boardroom - The Multifaceted Aspects of Digital Ready Boards,
Thinkingaire - 100 Game-Changing Digital Mindsets to Compete for the future,
Change Insight - Change as an Ongoing Capability to Fuel Digital Transformation,
IT Innovation - Reinvent IT for the Digital Age
Unpuzzling Innovation - Mastering Innovation in a Structural Way
and received very positive feedback.

Pearl is a digital visionary who can capture business insight, technology foresight, and perceive digital leadership and management philosophy from multi-dimensional lenses and global perspectives. She is also a forward-thinking digital leader who advocates business innovation and culture evolution.

Figure 10 The author's photo

Pearl is a prolific blogger who creates a professional and popular blog: "Future of CIO," which has reached the 3500+ posting milestones and catching 1,700, 000 + views from a worldwide audience. It covers more than 59+ hot IT and management subjects such as future of leadership, IT trends, digital transformation, organizational culture and management, business strategy and execution, innovation, IT transformation, Digital Master tuning, decision effectiveness, CIO Debate, Digital Transformation, Culture Master, talent management and risk intelligence, etc.

Pearl has worked for both Fortune 100 companies to gain a variety of experiences and startup to present entrepreneur spirit. Her cross-industrial, cross-functional and cross-cultural backgrounds make her a natural strategic and creative thinker, always see the other side of the coin, also inspire her to observe deeper and broader with the fresh eyes and open mind, to become a relentless change agent, the symbol of innovation, and a forward-looking digital leader.

She holds a master's degree in Computer Science from the University of Southern California, and she lives in San Francisco Bay Area for 15+ years.

www.ingramcontent.com/pod-product-compliance
Lightning Source LLC
Chambersburg PA
CBHW031945170526
45157CB00002B/393